Appium Insights

Strategies for Successful Platform Agnostic Test Automation

Sai Krishna V

Apress®

Appium Insights: Strategies for Successful Platform Agnostic Test Automation

Sai Krishna V
Bengaluru, Karnataka, India

ISBN-13 (pbk): 979-8-8688-1702-1   ISBN-13 (electronic): 979-8-8688-1703-8
https://doi.org/10.1007/979-8-8688-1703-8

Copyright © 2025 by Sai Krishna V

This work is subject to copyright. All rights are reserved by the Publisher, whether the whole or part of the material is concerned, specifically the rights of translation, reprinting, reuse of illustrations, recitation, broadcasting, reproduction on microfilms or in any other physical way, and transmission or information storage and retrieval, electronic adaptation, computer software, or by similar or dissimilar methodology now known or hereafter developed.

Trademarked names, logos, and images may appear in this book. Rather than use a trademark symbol with every occurrence of a trademarked name, logo, or image we use the names, logos, and images only in an editorial fashion and to the benefit of the trademark owner, with no intention of infringement of the trademark.

The use in this publication of trade names, trademarks, service marks, and similar terms, even if they are not identified as such, is not to be taken as an expression of opinion as to whether or not they are subject to proprietary rights.

While the advice and information in this book are believed to be true and accurate at the date of publication, neither the authors nor the editors nor the publisher can accept any legal responsibility for any errors or omissions that may be made. The publisher makes no warranty, express or implied, with respect to the material contained herein.

Managing Director, Apress Media LLC: Welmoed Spahr
Acquisitions Editor: Anandadeep Roy
Editorial Project Manager: Jessica Vakili

Distributed to the book trade worldwide by Springer Science+Business Media New York, 1 New York Plaza, New York, NY 10004. Phone 1-800-SPRINGER, fax (201) 348-4505, e-mail orders-ny@ springer-sbm.com, or visit www.springeronline.com. Apress Media, LLC is a Delaware LLC and the sole member (owner) is Springer Science + Business Media Finance Inc (SSBM Finance Inc). SSBM Finance Inc is a **Delaware** corporation.

For information on translations, please e-mail booktranslations@springernature.com; for reprint, paperback, or audio rights, please e-mail bookpermissions@springernature.com.

Apress titles may be purchased in bulk for academic, corporate, or promotional use. eBook versions and licenses are also available for most titles. For more information, reference our Print and eBook Bulk Sales web page at http://www.apress.com/bulk-sales.

Any source code or other supplementary material referenced by the author in this book is available to readers on GitHub. For more detailed information, please visit https://www.apress.com/gp/services/source-code.

If disposing of this product, please recycle the paper

To my parents, Mr. Vijaya Kumar and Mrs. Meena Kumari, for their unwavering support; to my wife Priya and son Kiaan, who make every day meaningful; to the open source community that has shaped my journey; and to my partners in open source for nearly a decade, Srinivasan Sekar and Jaydeep Chakrabarty, whose collaboration has made this work possible.

Table of Contents

About the Author xiii

About the Technical Reviewers xv

Acknowledgments xvii

Foreword xix

Chapter 1: Introduction to Appium 3.0 1
   The Birth of Appium 1
      Initial Exploration 1
      Creation of iOS Auto 1
      The Turning Point: Selenium Conference 2012 2
      Open Source Release and Evolution 2
      Project Naming 2
      Growth and Community Involvement 2
   What Is Appium Used For? 3
   Appium Architecture 3
      Standardization of Automation for Mobile Applications 3
      Extensibility and Platform Support 4
      Appium's Client-Server Architecture 4
   A Closer Look at Appium Plugin 6
      Enhanced Workflow with Plugins 7
      Plugin Processing 7
   Exploring Appium Drivers 8
   Plugins and Drivers Maintained by Appium Team and Community 9
   Key Benefits of Appium 3.0 10
   Summary 11

TABLE OF CONTENTS

Chapter 2: Getting Started with Appium 3.0 13

Module Introduction 13

What You Will Learn 13

The Importance of a Solid Foundation 14

Prerequisites for Appium 14

Installing Node.js 15

Java Development Kit (JDK) 16

    Step 1: Download and Install JDK 16

    Step 2: Set Up the JAVA_HOME Environment Variable 16

    Step 3: Verify JAVA_HOME Setup 17

    Step 4: Verify JDK Installation 17

Appium Server Installation 17

    Step 1: Open a Terminal or Command Prompt 17

    Step 2: Verify the Appium Installation 18

Android-Specific Prerequisites 18

    Install Android Studio for Mac 19

    Install Android Studio for Windows 24

    Set Up Environment Variables for Windows 24

    Set Up Environment Variables for Mac/Linux 25

    Verify ANDROID_HOME 26

    Working with Emulators 26

iOS-Specific Prerequisites 27

    Install Xcode on Mac 27

    Install Xcode Command-Line Tools 28

Appium Driver Installation 30

    Listing Supported Drivers 30

    Install Drivers 31

Appium Plugin Installation 36

Listing Supported Plugins...36

    Listing Supported Plugins...36
    Install Plugins 37
    Appium Doctor..40
  Summary..42

Chapter 3: Real Device Configuration 43

  Module Introduction..43
  What You Will Learn 43
  Setup Android Real Device..44
  Setup iOS Real Device...45
  WebDriverAgent for Real Device 50
    What Is WebDriverAgent?...50
    How Does WebDriverAgent Work?..50
    How to Build WebDriverAgent?...51
    Steps to Create a WebDriverAgent IPA 54
  Summary..61

Chapter 4: All About Desired Capabilities 63

  What Will You Learn 63
  What Are Desired Capabilities?...63
  Types of Capabilities 64
    1. Standard Capabilities 64
    2. Appium-Specific Capabilities...64
    3. Cloud-Specific Capabilities..65
    4. Mandatory Capabilities..65
    5. Cloud Provider Integration 65
  Capabilities for Parallel Execution 66
    1. Per-Process Approach 66
    2. Per-Request Approach (Preferred Method)...67
    3. Key Capabilities for Parallel Execution 67
    4. Best Practices for Parallel Execution...68
  Summary..68

TABLE OF CONTENTS

Chapter 5: How to Inspect Elements 71

What Will You Learn 71

How to Install Inspector 71

Create a Session for Android and iOS 73

    Why Use Cloud Devices? 78

Exploring Appium Inspector 82

    View the Mobile App Hierarchy 83

    Selecting Elements for Android 83

    Recommended Locator Strategies for Android 84

    Selecting Elements for iOS 85

    Recommended Locator Strategies for iOS 88

    Element Interaction with Inspector 89

Summary 92

Chapter 6: Writing First Test 95

What Will You Learn 95

Setting Up the Environment 95

WDIO Project Setup 95

    Initialize a New WDIO Project 96

    Install WebdriverIO and Required Packages 96

    Run the WDIO Configuration Wizard 97

    Creating Separate wdio.config.ts Files for Android and iOS 100

Summary 105

Chapter 7: Understand Appium Logs 107

What Will You Learn 107

Introduction to Appium Server Logs 107

    Breaking Down the Android Logs 107

    Understanding iOS Server Logs 116

Summary 125

Chapter 8: All You Need to Know on Gestures 127

What We Will Learn 127

WebDriver Specification: Actions API 127

How to Perform a Gesture in Detail 128

    Interpreting the Gesture from the Image in Figure 8-2 129

Step-by-Step Breakdown of the Code 130

Other Ways to Perform a Gesture 131

Summary 133

Chapter 9: Build Appium Plugin 135

What We Will Learn 135

What the Plugin Can Do? 135

Create Project Skeleton 136

    Step 1: Initialize the Project 136

    Step 2: Update package.json 136

    Step 3: Install Dependencies 137

    Step 4: Create the Plugin Class 137

Intercept and Handle Specific Appium Commands 138

    How to Identify Supported Command Names? 138

    Understanding Command Method Parameters 138

Intercepting and Handling All Appium Commands 140

    Parameters of the handle Method 140

    Example: Logging Command Execution Time 141

Adding CLI Arguments to the Appium Plugin 145

Overloading Execute Script 147

    How the Execute Script Command Works in WebDriver 147

    How the Execute Method Works in Appium 147

    How Plugin Overrides Work 150

Add Custom Plugin Scripts 150

Summary 151

TABLE OF CONTENTS

Chapter 10: Optimizing and Troubleshooting Appium Tests 153

What You Will Learn 153

Performance Optimization for iOS Real Device Tests 153

    Prebuild WebDriverAgent 154

    Setting Up WebDriverAgent 154

    WebDriverAgent Initialization and Connectivity 155

    Making WDA Readiness in Node.js 155

Handling OTP Field Input Using W3C Actions 158

Using W3C Actions for OTP Input 158

Tap on Element at Specific Location 159

Capturing Multiple Screenshots Efficiently in Test Execution 160

Enabling MJPEG Server for Faster Screenshots 161

Managing Contexts in Appium 161

    Key Considerations When Managing Contexts 164

How to Manage Locators in React Native App 165

    Platform-Specific Mappings 166

    Key Conflicts 166

    Robust Solution 166

Chapter 11: Contribute to Appium 169

What You Will Learn 169

Appium's Monorepo Structure 169

Core Architecture Components 170

The Command Execution Flow 177

Extension System: Drivers and Plugins 179

    Drivers 179

    Plugins 180

HTTP Server and Routing 181

Session Management 182

Bidirectional (BiDi) Communication 182

End-to-End Flow: Creating an Android Session 183

TABLE OF CONTENTS

    Client-Side Initialization 183

    Driver Hierarchy for Android Automation 184

Session Initialization Process 185

Communication with the Device 186

Building Appium Locally 187

    1. Clone the Appium Repository 188

    2. Install Dependencies 188

    3. Build the Appium Server 188

    4. Clone and Build a Driver (e.g., UIAutomator2) 189

Summary 192

Chapter 12: Integrating Appium Tests in Continuous Integration (CI) Pipelines 193

What Will You Learn 193

    The Importance of CI in Mobile Test Automation 193

How to Run Appium Tests in GitHub Actions 194

    Android GitHub Actions YAML 194

    iOS GitHub YAML File 199

Summary 204

Index 205

About the Author

Sai Krishna is a seasoned test automation architect and Director of Engineering at LambdaTest India. As a proficient conference speaker and dedicated blogger, Sai has showcased his expertise in various renowned events such as SeleniumConf, AppiumConf, TestMu Conference, and Belgrade Test Conference. Passionate about fostering local tech communities, organizing events, and promoting thought leadership, Sai is not only an active contributor but also a fervent open source evangelist. His contributions span across projects like Appium, Selenium, WebdriverIO, and more, solidifying his reputation as a prominent figure in the testing and automation domain.

About the Technical Reviewers

Srinivasan Sekar serves as the Director of Engineering at LambdaTest. A passionate advocate for open source, he is a recognized Appium member and an active contributor to several prominent repositories, including Selenium, WebdriverIO, and Taiko. With deep expertise in testing microservices, event-driven applications, and both mobile and web platforms, Srinivasan is known for his skill in building robust automation frameworks. He has also shared his insights at numerous industry conferences such as SeleniumConf, AppiumConf, Agile India, XConf Singapore, Quest4Quality, BelgradeTestConf, FOSDEM, HUSTEF, and Nordic Testing Days conference.

Mykola Mokhnach began his career in 2003 in Kyiv, Ukraine, where he balanced university studies with a part-time job at a tech startup. Over the years, he explored various career paths, experimenting with different technologies and even taking a brief detour into management. In 2014, he joined a Berlin-based startup as an Automation Engineer, which marked the beginning of his journey into mobile automation. It was there that he first contributed to the Appium open source project—a path he's been on ever since.

Since 2016, he's had the privilege of working alongside the talented Appium team, and he takes great pride in both contributing to its ongoing success and sharing his knowledge with the global community of mobile automation practitioners.

Acknowledgments

First and foremost, I want to express my deepest gratitude to the team at Apress. Without their guidance and support, this book would not have been possible. I also extend my sincere thanks to Srinivasan Sekar and Mykola Mokhnach, who served as technical reviewers and testers, ensuring the accuracy and quality of the content on Appium.

This book reveals hidden treasures about Appium internals and provides a roadmap for those looking to contribute to the repository. I am deeply grateful to Jonathan Lipps for writing the foreword to this book and for lighting the path for many engineers like myself.

Finally, I want to express my heartfelt gratitude to my wife, Priya, for her unwavering support throughout this entire writing journey. Her encouragement made all the difference.

Foreword

Jonathan Lipps - Appium Technical Architect.

Mobile app testing keeps getting more complex, having a comprehensive and practical guide is invaluable. What sets this book apart is not just the depth of technical knowledge it contains, but the clarity with which Sai distills complex concepts into actionable insights. His years of hands-on experience and teaching shine through every chapter.

Mobile test automation demands more than just technical proficiency. It requires strategic thinking about test architecture, framework design, and maintainability. Sai addresses these critical dimensions, guiding readers through essential strategies such as choosing the right locator approaches, implementing robust wait mechanisms, designing scalable page object models, and handling the complexities of cross-platform testing. He also covers real-world challenges, from managing flaky tests to optimizing test execution across diverse device farms, that help readers to deal with a variety of roadblocks including fragmented device ecosystems and unexpected network conditions. As an Appium community contributor and veteran teacher, Sai guides readers gently through both foundational and advanced scenarios.

Whether you're a QA professional taking your first steps with Appium, a developer looking to strengthen your testing capabilities, or a seasoned automation engineer seeking to refine your mobile testing strategies, you'll find this book to be an indispensable companion. It's more than a technical manual. It's a distillation of years of real-world experience, community engagement, and a genuine passion for helping others succeed in mobile test automation.

FOREWORD

Asad Khan CEO and Co-Founder of LambdaTest.

The mobile testing landscape has undergone a remarkable transformation over the past decade. What once required extensive physical device labs and complex infrastructure can now be executed at scale through cloud-based platforms. Yet, despite these technological advances, the fundamental challenges of mobile testing remain: ensuring app quality across fragmented ecosystems, managing testing complexity, and delivering exceptional user experiences.

At LambdaTest, we work with thousands of development and QA teams worldwide, and we've witnessed firsthand the challenges they face in mobile testing. The complexity of modern mobile applications, combined with the fragmentation of devices, operating systems, network conditions, and platform-specific behaviors, makes comprehensive testing both critical and challenging. Teams struggle with issues ranging from test instability and poor test coverage to lengthy feedback cycles and inadequate testing strategies for native, hybrid, and cross-platform applications.

This is why Sai's book is so timely and valuable. Having collaborated with the Appium community for years, Sai brings a practitioner's perspective that goes beyond theoretical knowledge. His approach addresses the real-world challenges that teams encounter in mobile testing. What sets this book apart is how Sai helps readers understand not just the "how" but the "why" behind effective mobile test automation. He excels at helping you identify where problems truly live—whether it's in your test architecture, your element location strategy, your wait mechanisms, or your overall testing approach.

The book is rich with real-world examples drawn from actual production scenarios. Sai doesn't just present abstract concepts; he walks you through practical situations you'll encounter in your testing journey. His discussion of test architecture goes beyond simple patterns, exploring how to build maintainable, scalable frameworks that can evolve with your application.

What impresses me most about this work is its comprehensive approach to mobile testing strategy. Modern mobile testing isn't just about automation; it's about understanding the unique characteristics of mobile platforms, knowing when and what to automate, designing effective test suites that balance coverage and execution time, and building resilient systems that provide reliable feedback. Sai's treatment of these topics reflects a deep understanding of the mobile testing lifecycle, from test design and implementation to execution, reporting, and continuous improvement.

CHAPTER 1

Introduction to Appium 3.0

The Birth of Appium

Back in 2011, Dan who was a test manager at Zoosk faced a big issue. The length of test passes on their iOS product was getting out of hand. While reducing testing could have been considered, it posed more risks. Dan thought about automating the testing process for iOS apps.

Initial Exploration

Dan began by looking at the existing mobile application automation tools, only to find out they have major disadvantages. For instance, testing was only done using Apple's UIAutomation which required writing code using JavaScript, and there were no real-time debugging abilities. As a result, tests had to be done inside Xcode's profiling instruments so as not to complicate things further.

Despite such limitations, he saw a way through based on this current technology. He ended up producing a "working" solution although it was inexecutable on real devices among other problems. This led him to the idea of running the UIAutomation framework in real time like an interpreter.

Creation of iOS Auto

Here, he tried to experiment if it's possible to run UIAutomation in real-time mode by taking commands from the UIAutomation JavaScript program and execute them back within it. Through writing out shell scripts which were put together in a certain order, he came up with a prototype that he called iOS Auto.

CHAPTER 1   INTRODUCTION TO APPIUM 3.0

The Turning Point: Selenium Conference 2012

During the 2012 Selenium Conference, Dan introduced iOS Auto. There was so much enthusiasm in the audience about using Selenium syntax for mobile automation. This cool test architecture became a hot talk with several people suggesting that he make a lightning talk about it.

At the conference, Dan met Jason Huggins who was moderating the lightning talks. iOS Auto intrigued Jason because he realized it could automate iPhones. Thus began a very important collaboration between these two men.

Open Source Release and Evolution

Therefore, in August 2012, advised by long-time open source promoter Jason, Dan published iOS Auto code on GitHub under a permissive OSS license. Seeing the advantage of this, Jason made it possible to write iOS Auto scripts from any client library for selenium WebDriver by adding a web server and implementing WebDriver protocols over HTTP. This then made the project independent of its choice of language.

Project Naming

Subsequently, during the course of project development, Dan and Jason brainstormed on the suitable name. Having thought of "Apple Cart" initially, the idea was scratched over his fears concerning Apple's trademarks. Finally, "Appium" became their final decision signifying "Selenium" for applications.

Growth and Community Involvement

From there, they passed it over to Jonathan who took over as an architect, thus leading into a new phase. Appium 1.0's release took place in May 2014 through Jonathan Lipps. Thus, over the next decade, it grew and continued with support from its fertile community after which in 2023 came Appium 2.0, which opened up a broader system focus rather than being narrowly just one project.

What Is Appium Used For?

Appium is an open source, cross-platform test automation tool designed for native and hybrid mobile applications. In addition to mobile apps, Appium supports testing for desktop applications, TV OS, Unity games, and many other applications, depending on the drivers developed for it.

Appium 1.0's core philosophy has been preserved in Appium 2.0 such that it does not expect users to recompile or modify their applications in order to test them. The use of standard automation APIs means seamless integration between different platforms. Since it supports any WebDriver-compatible language like Java, Python, Ruby, C#, and Node.js, it allows developers to write their tests.

Any testing framework is a customer's choice. For those who like Java, one can use JUnit or TestNG, while others might prefer Mocha and Jasmine among other running tools if they are fond of Node.js. This in-built feature of Appium helps users easily switch back and forth from testing native apps to WebViews on the same page, thus ensuring a broad range of testing.

Appium Architecture

Appium relies on WebDriver protocol, a technology that has for a long time been the leading one in the realm of UI automation. The main objective of WebDriver has always been to focus on automating web browser's UIs which in essence is just a subset of what Appium is meant for. Selenium is fundamentally designed for web UI automation, while Appium intends to make the same possible but for mobile apps as well as beyond these.

Through involvement with different web browser manufacturers and standard bodies such as W3C, Selenium has made its API a recognized web standard platform called the WebDriver specification. When it comes to the issue of standardization, Appium decided to utilize this spec too so that its automation API is aligned with that of WebDriver.

Standardization of Automation for Mobile Applications

Initially, Appium set out on its mission to create a mobile application automation standard with special emphasis on iOS and Android. As opposed to coming up with a new standard from zero, the core team adopted an extension of the WebDriver specification (Note: This) for their project which did not only guarantee them adherence to established norms but also enabled support for certain exclusive mobile behaviors not related to browsers, that is, native mobile commands.

Extensibility and Platform Support

In this framework, Appium can run on a variety of platforms like mobile devices, TV OS, and even Raspberry Pi by implementing the WebDriver specification as its base. Appium provides device-specific interactions through the extensibility of WebDriver specs and adheres to the same structure in its API.

Appium's Client-Server Architecture

Appium is built on a client-server architecture where transactions are conducted using HTTP protocols, as shown in Figure 1-1.

CHAPTER 1   INTRODUCTION TO APPIUM 3.0

Figure 1-1. *Architecture of Appium workflow for iOS and Android*

Here's how the architecture works:

- **Client**: For example, your test code would be a client that can be written in any WebDriver-compatible language, such as Java, Python, Ruby, C#, or JavaScript (using WebdriverIO).The usual tasks related to the client code are mostly about creating sessions, finding elements, and thus interacting with these elements.

5

- **Server**: The Appium server interprets requests from a client and identifies if it is for iOS or Android.

- **Driver**: Internally, it uses the WebDriver protocol to forward requests correctly. XCUITest driver takes care of iOS while Espresso or UIAutomator2 driver handles Android requests.

- **Device Servers**: Each driver communicates with a server that is located on the device itself. WebDriverAgent is used for iOS, while UIAutomator2 server and Espresso server are used for Android.

These servers are standalone applications on devices, making it possible for direct user interface component interaction.

Client-to-Device Process Flow

Overcoming the specifics in order to work with each driver, Appium server sends the request from the client identifying its device target platform in terms of Android or iOS. The driver sends commands to start the server, which executes them finding elements, scrolling, or other user actions based on the request. In case the driver cannot process the request further, third-party libraries or native tools such as ADB, go-ios, and ios-deploy might be employed.

Appium server and Appium client do not need to be running on the same machine. You simply need to be able to make a HTTP request from the client to the server over some network.

A Closer Look at Appium Plugin

The Appium plugin stands as a form of extension mechanism that allows for the enhancement or customization of the primary operations found within the Appium server. For instance, the plugin could introduce new commands and change existing commands within an operation or even the way that Appium itself performs some duties. Due to this modularity, developers find building automation testing environments that are geared toward specific requirements much easier without having to change the core Appium codebase. Figure 1-2 shows how the Appium architecture changes when the plugin is activated alongside Appium.

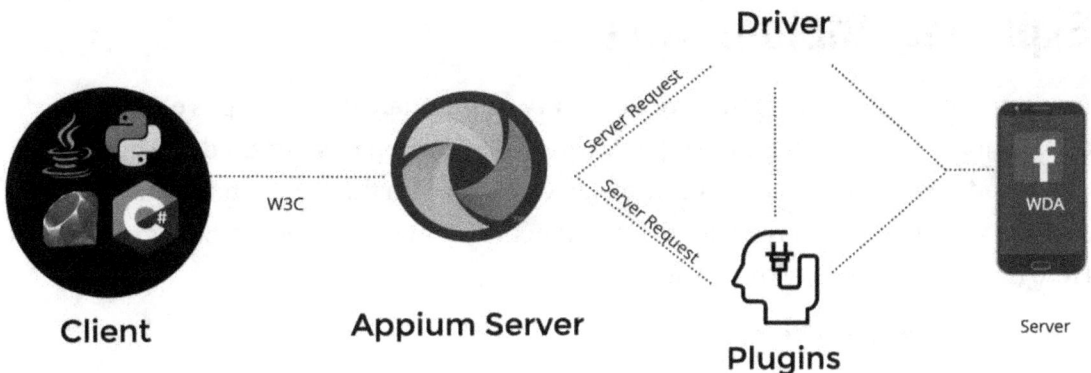

Figure 1-2. *Architecture of plugin*

Enhanced Workflow with Plugins

If you activate a plugin in an Appium server, the base plugin will know which methods it has to intercept. For example, let's see what happens when a "createSession" request is made from the client after activating a plugin; here, the plugin has implemented the "createSession."

Plugin Processing

In this case, the plugin intercepts the "createSession" request from the client. The plugin will then process the request before deciding what next steps should be taken. There are two cases:

1. **Forward to Drivers**: At times, the plugin decides to forward such requests to their respective drivers for further action.

2. **Handle Internally**: Other times, the plugin may choose to handle this request by itself and send the response back to the server.

CHAPTER 1   INTRODUCTION TO APPIUM 3.0

Exploring Appium Drivers

Appium drivers are plugins that are necessary to automate various types of mobile applications. Appium does not ship with any drivers when it is installed, so one must download them separately. In Appium 2.0, you start with the simple base version of Appium and then install relevant drivers depending on what needs to be automated. Here is what you need to know about them:

1. Pluggable drivers

   - Unlike most testing frameworks, Appium does not contain any default test drivers.
   - Appropriate drivers must be installed based on the platform (Android, iOS, etc.) and actual automation engine to be used.

2. Driver installation

   - These are the drivers one would need:
     - For Android, you might consider between an Espresso driver and UIAutomator2 driver.
     - For iOS, however, you would have no other choice but to go with XCUITest driver.
     - Other community-driven platforms provide some drivers meant for their unique needs like Appium Unity driver which helps Unity-based applications.

3. Driver responsibilities

   - Each driver must implement an internal Appium interface that represents the WebDriver protocol.
   - Automation strategies vary greatly across different platforms due to freedom in implementing these restriction types by the driver developers.

4. Independent modules

    – One of the design aspects was that each driver should be autonomous so that they can be made individually just in case there are any changes in operating systems supported by each of these drivers, hence meeting the needs of every client separately.

    – For this kind of a scenario, it is only the modules used for automation that are attached to the software while ignoring the rest.

5. Usage

    – After the installation process has been completed, a user can start an Appium server and enable the driver they need to use for the automation of a particular kind of software on the given platform.

Plugins and Drivers Maintained by Appium Team and Community

Appium, the versatile automation framework, offers a range of drivers and plugins to cater to various testing needs. Each driver and plugin is maintained by different teams and contributors, ensuring the robust and seamless operation of the framework. Below is the list of some key drivers and plugins in the Appium ecosystem maintained by the community and the dev team.

Table 1-1. Drivers and Plugins List

Name	Type	Maintained by
UIAutomator2	Driver	Appium team
XCUITest	Driver	Appium team
Espresso	Driver	Appium team
Chromium	Driver	Appium team
Gecko	Driver	Appium team
Appium Flutter Integration	Driver	AppiumTestDistribution
Execute	Plugin	Appium team
Relaxed caps	Plugin	Appium team
Images	Plugin	Appium team
Universal XML	Plugin	Appium team
Appium Device Farm	Plugin	AppiumTestDistribution
Appium Wait	Plugin	AppiumTestDistribution
Appium Installer	Plugin	AppiumTestDistribution
Gesture	Plugin	AppiumTestDistribution
Appium ocr	Plugin	jlipps
Appium Interceptor	Plugin	AppiumTestDistribution
Appium DDlog	Plugin	rerorero
Appium Altunity	Plugin	headspinio

Key Benefits of Appium 3.0

Appium 3.0 brings significant advancements to the test automation landscape, offering enhanced flexibility, customization, and efficiency. Below are the key benefits that make Appium a game-changer for automation testing:

1. **Modular Driver Architecture**
   - **Custom Driver Creation**: This will enable you to create drivers specifically for the automation you desire, hence enhancing more control and customizations.
   - **Driver Installation Flexibility**: Only install drivers required for test automation, hence saving space, thus increasing effectiveness.

2. **Plugin Support**
   - **Custom Plugins**: Make your own plugins in order to add more specific actions and features that are not available in ordinary automation on top of extending Appium's capabilities.

3. **Streamlined Configuration**
   - **What You Ask Is What You Get**: Optimize your test environment by selecting only essential drivers and plugins, leaving out any other unwanted components.

Summary

Appium: Origins and Evolution traces the foundational facets of Appium. Appium's origin was in 2011 when Dan Cuellar thought about it. He had been experiencing slow test runs on Zoosk's iOS products until he thought about Appium. He called it iOS Auto and presented it in 2012 at the Selenium Conference by Dan. Later, he teamed up with Jason Huggins, who they decided to make it free for everyone else known as Appium. From then until now, there are a number of contributors who have done various things like improving documentation or fixing bugs, especially those related to platforms other than iOS.

Appium lets you test native, hybrid, and mobile web applications on different platforms such as mobile devices (iOS or Android), desktop applications, TV OS, etc. Designed as an automation tool but being versatile, open source Appium employs client-server architecture using WebDriver protocols for cross-platform automation of mobile applications. In it, there are the Appium server, clients (WDIO, Java client), drivers, and

CHAPTER 1   INTRODUCTION TO APPIUM 3.0

servers–all integrated well within a single suite connected through common APIs, so they work each other out smoothly making sure no problems emerge while running tests against real devices or emulators.

Appium drivers are essential for automating different types of applications. Users must install appropriate drivers based on the target platform, such as UIAutomator2 for Android and XCUITest for iOS. The Appium ecosystem includes various plugins and drivers maintained by the Appium team and the community. These plugins extend Appium's capabilities, enabling customized automation scenarios. Appium introduces a modular driver architecture, plugin support, and streamlined configuration, offering enhanced flexibility, customization, and efficiency in automation testing.

In the next chapter, we will be discussing how you can begin setting up your environment for Appium, including installation procedures, configuration settings, and some basic test scripts that we will use in the initial stages of mobile automation testing.

CHAPTER 2

Getting Started with Appium 3.0

Module Introduction

In the previous chapter, we already looked at why Appium and its importance. However, before diving into writing test scripts, it is crucial to ensure that your environment is properly set up. A misconfigured environment can lead to frustrating errors and wasted time, making it essential to get this first step right. This chapter will guide you through the initial setup process, helping you avoid common pitfalls and ensuring that your Appium journey starts on the right foot.

What You Will Learn

In this chapter, we will cover the essential prerequisites and setup steps required to get Appium 3.0 up and running on your machine. We'll start by discussing the necessary operating system and software requirements, ensuring that your environment is well equipped to support mobile automation. From there, we'll introduce you to Appium Doctor, a valuable tool that helps verify your setup and diagnose potential issues before they become roadblocks.

Next, we'll walk you through the installation of Appium 3.0 using Node Package Manager (NPM), the industry-standard package manager for JavaScript. This section will provide clear, step-by-step instructions to ensure that the installation process is smooth and error-free.

CHAPTER 2   GETTING STARTED WITH APPIUM 3.0

Once Appium is installed, we'll explore the various drivers that Appium supports, such as UiAutomator2 for Android and XCUITest for iOS. You'll learn how to install and configure these drivers, as well as how to choose the right driver for your specific automation needs.

Additionally, we'll introduce you to the world of Appium plugins. These plugins extend Appium's capabilities, allowing you to customize and enhance your automation framework. We'll guide you through the process of installing and configuring plugins, with practical examples to illustrate their use.

The Importance of a Solid Foundation

The "Getting Started with Appium 3.0" chapter is not just about installing software—it's about laying the groundwork for successful mobile automation. A well-configured environment ensures that your test scripts run smoothly, reducing the time spent troubleshooting and increasing the time spent on actual test development. By the end of this chapter, you will have a fully functional Appium environment, ready to handle the complexities of mobile testing.

Prerequisites for Appium

To install Appium, you will need to meet several prerequisites, depending on whether you are setting up for Android, iOS, or both.

General Prerequisites

1. **Node.js**: Appium is built on Node.js, so you need to have it installed.

   - **Recommended Version**: Node.js LTS.
   - Install Node.js from `https://nodejs.org/en/download/package-manager`.

2. **Java Development Kit (JDK)**: Required for running Appium and Android testing.

   - Install **JDK 11** or later (recommended: **JDK 17**).
   - Set up the JAVA_HOME environment variable pointing to your JDK installation.

3. **Appium Server**: This is the core component of Appium.

CHAPTER 2   GETTING STARTED WITH APPIUM 3.0

Android-Specific Prerequisites

1. **Android SDK**: Required for Android testing.

2. **Emulator or Real Device**: You'll need either an Android emulator or a real device for testing.

3. **ADB**: Android Debug Bridge (ADB) should be accessible via the command line.

iOS-Specific Prerequisites

1. **macOS**: iOS testing can only be done on macOS.

2. **Xcode**: Required for building and running iOS apps.

3. **iOS real devices or iOS simulators**

Installing Node.js

You can download Node.js by nvm where you can manage multiple versions in an ease of use Prebuild Installer which is always one version.

Recommended way is through nvm as follows. Refer to Figure 2-1.

```
# install nvm (Node Version Manager)
$ curl -o- https://raw.githubusercontent.com/nvm-sh/nvm/v0.40.0/install.sh | bash
# download and install Node.js(you may need to restart the terminal)
nvm install 22
# verifies the right Node.js versios is in the environment
node -v # should print `v22.20.0`
# verifies the right npm version is in the environment
npm -v # should print `10.9.3`
```

Figure 2-1. *Installing node via nvm*

CHAPTER 2   GETTING STARTED WITH APPIUM 3.0

Java Development Kit (JDK)

Step 1: Download and Install JDK

- **Windows/Mac/Linux**

    1. Visit the Oracle JDK download page (https://www.oracle.com/java/technologies/javase-jdk17-downloads.html).

    2. Download the appropriate installer for your operating system (JDK 17 is recommended).

    3. Follow the installation instructions provided by the installer.

Step 2: Set Up the JAVA_HOME Environment Variable

- **Windows**

    1. Right-click "This PC" or "Computer" on your desktop or in File Explorer.

    2. Select "Properties."

    3. Click "Advanced system settings."

    4. Click the "Environment Variables" button.

    5. Under "System Variables," click "New" and enter the following:

        - **Variable name**: JAVA_HOME

        - **Variable value**: Path to your JDK installation (e.g., C:\Program Files\Java\jdk-17)

    6. Click "OK" to save the changes.

- **Mac/Linux**

    1. Open a terminal and edit your shell profile (e.g., .bashrc, .bash_profile, or .zshrc) by running: nano ~/.bash_profile

CHAPTER 2   GETTING STARTED WITH APPIUM 3.0

2. Add the following line at the end of the file: export JAVA_HOME=$(/usr/libexec/java_home -v 17)

3. Save the file and reload the shell profile: source ~/.bash_profile

Step 3: Verify JAVA_HOME Setup

Open a terminal or command prompt and run: echo $JAVA_HOME.

- It should print the path to your JDK installation directory. Refer to Figure 2-2.

Step 4: Verify JDK Installation

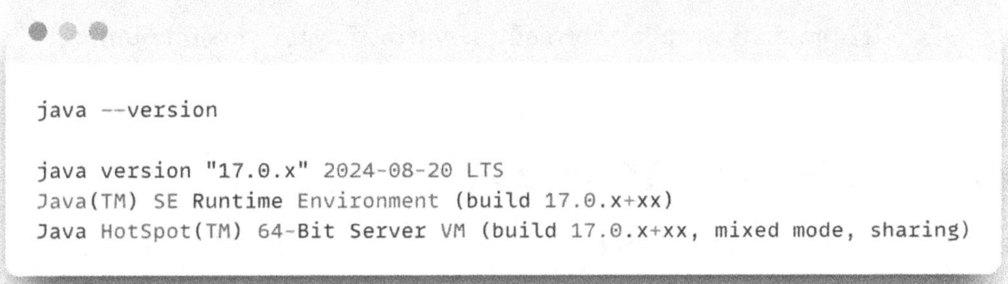

```
java --version

java version "17.0.x" 2024-08-20 LTS
Java(TM) SE Runtime Environment (build 17.0.x+xx)
Java HotSpot(TM) 64-Bit Server VM (build 17.0.x+xx, mixed mode, sharing)
```

Figure 2-2. *Check installed java version*

Appium Server Installation

Step 1: Open a Terminal or Command Prompt

Run the following command to install Appium globally as in Figure 2-3.

CHAPTER 2   GETTING STARTED WITH APPIUM 3.0

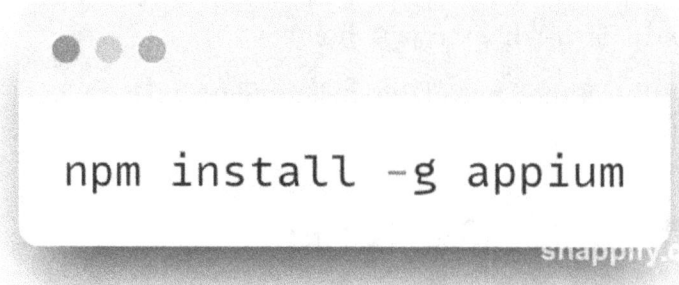

Figure 2-3. *Installing Appium globally*

Step 2: Verify the Appium Installation

1. **Verify Installation**

    - Run `appium -v` to check the installed version of Appium.

    - If Appium is installed correctly, it will display the version number.

Android-Specific Prerequisites

With our foundational setup in place, it's time to turn our focus to Android-specific configurations. As we dive deeper into the world of mobile testing, being equipped to test on both emulators and real devices is essential. Android, being one of the most widely used mobile operating systems globally, offers a robust and versatile environment for app development and testing.

In this section, we will guide you through the process of installing the necessary tools and software to create a fully functional Android testing environment. Whether you're aiming to run tests on virtual devices (emulators) or actual physical devices, the steps we cover will ensure that you're well prepared for both scenarios.

By the end of this module, you will have

- Installed Android Studio, which comes bundled with the Android SDK.

- Configured the Android SDK to include essential tools for development and testing.

CHAPTER 2 GETTING STARTED WITH APPIUM 3.0

- Set up environment variables to streamline command-line operations.
- Verified your installation to ensure everything is functioning correctly.

Install Android Studio for Mac

1. **Download Android Studio**
   - Visit the official Android Studio download page and download the installer for your operating system and install the studio.
2. Open Finder and go to Applications folder. Double-click Android Studio and select Create a new project. Refer to Figure 2-4.

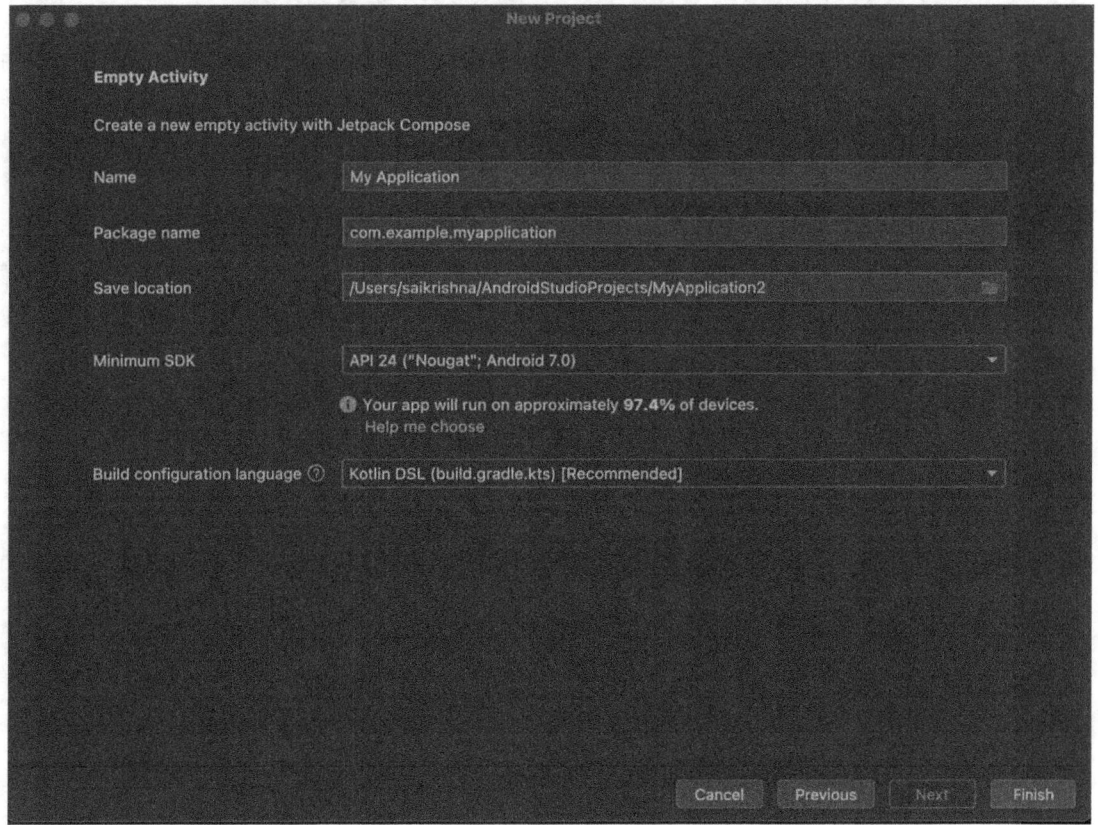

Figure 2-4. *Create empty Android project*

CHAPTER 2 GETTING STARTED WITH APPIUM 3.0

3. Click the Finish button and wait for the required dependencies to download.

4. Click the Finish button again and you should see the application project in Android Studio; wait until all the Gradle dependencies are downloaded.

5. Now we need to create an emulator for our testing as per Figure 2-5.

    1. Select Device Manager.

    2. Click Add a New Device.

    3. Select Create a Virtual Device. Refer to Figure 2-6.

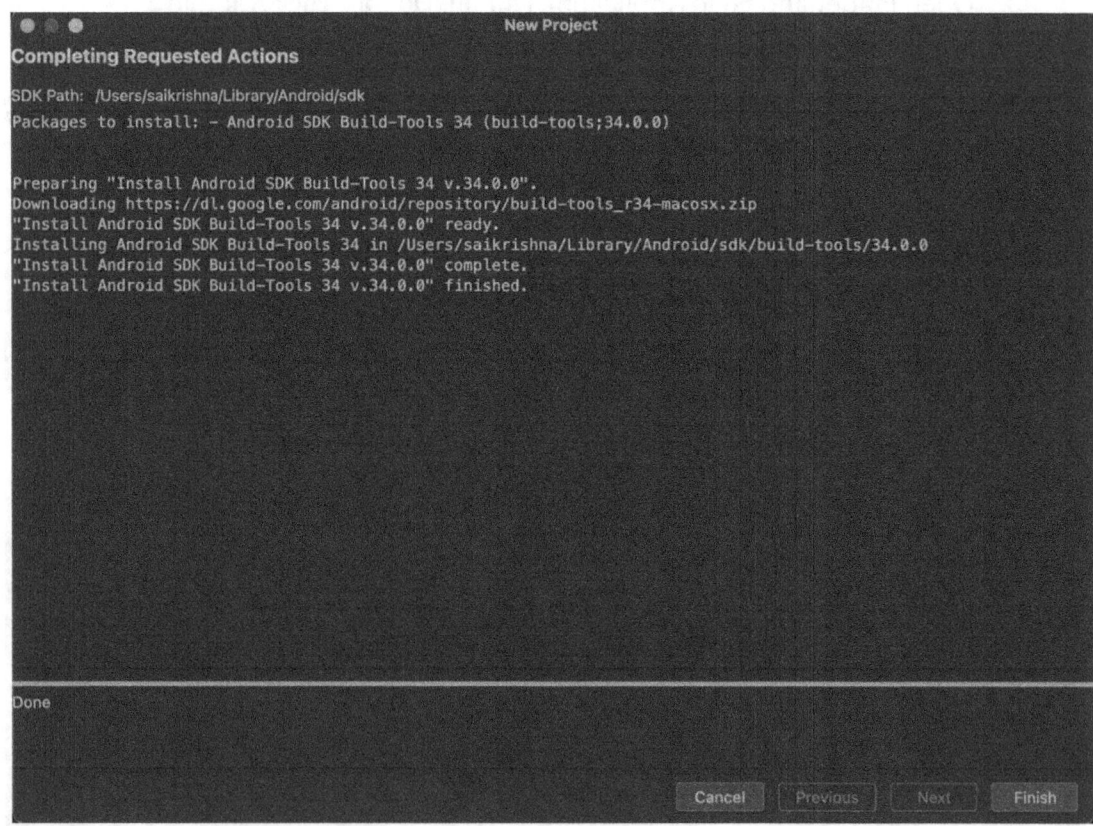

Figure 2-5. *Download Android SDK build*

CHAPTER 2   GETTING STARTED WITH APPIUM 3.0

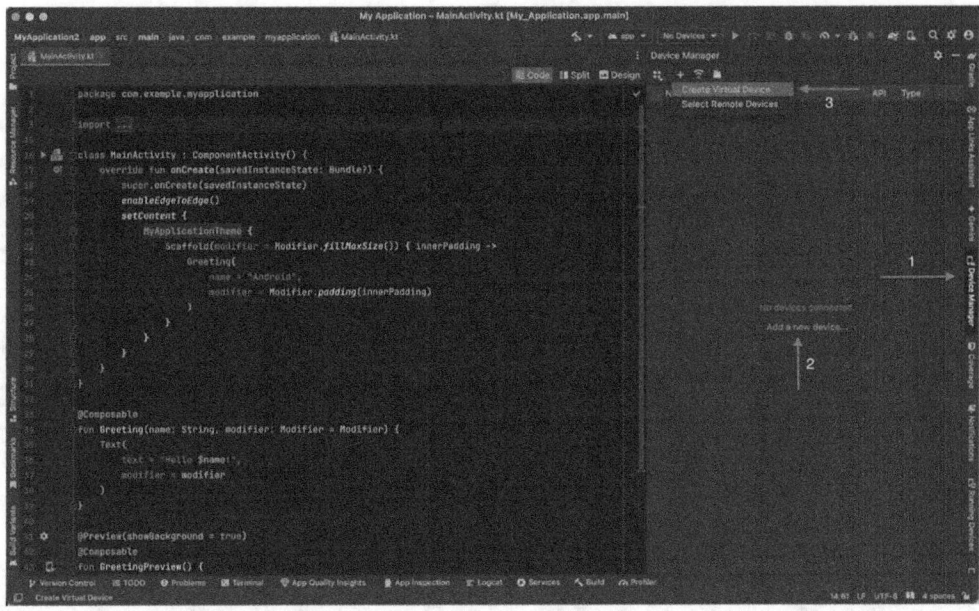

Figure 2-6. *Creating virtual device*

6. Choose any Device Configuration and click Next. Refer to Figure 2-7.

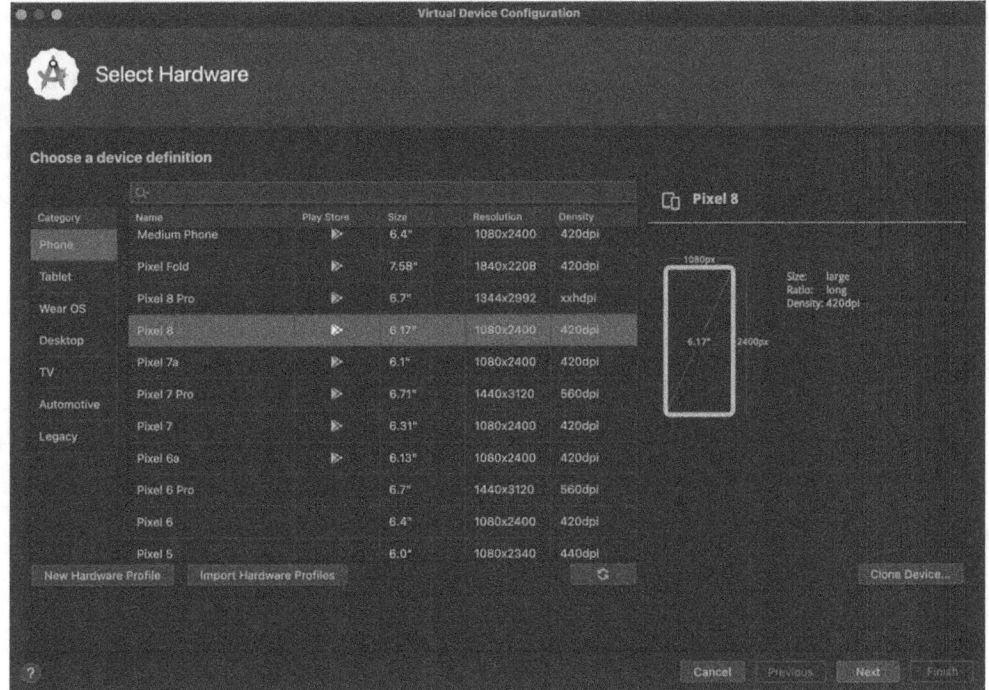

Figure 2-7. *Choose Select Device Hardware*

21

7. Download any of the recommended image. We will select API 34 and wait for all required dependencies to finish downloading. Once all is done, click Finish button and then you should see the Next button getting enabled. Refer to Figure 2-8.

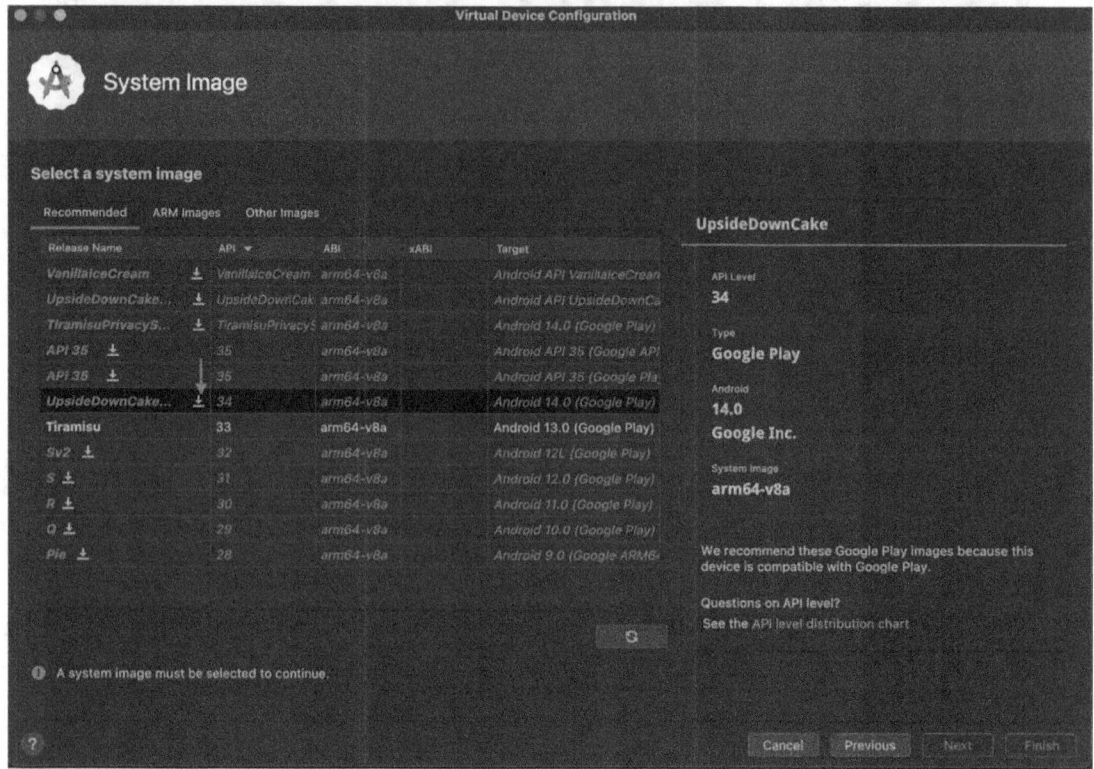

Figure 2-8. Download System Image

8. Set an AVD name of your choice and click Finish button. Refer to Figure 2-9.

CHAPTER 2 GETTING STARTED WITH APPIUM 3.0

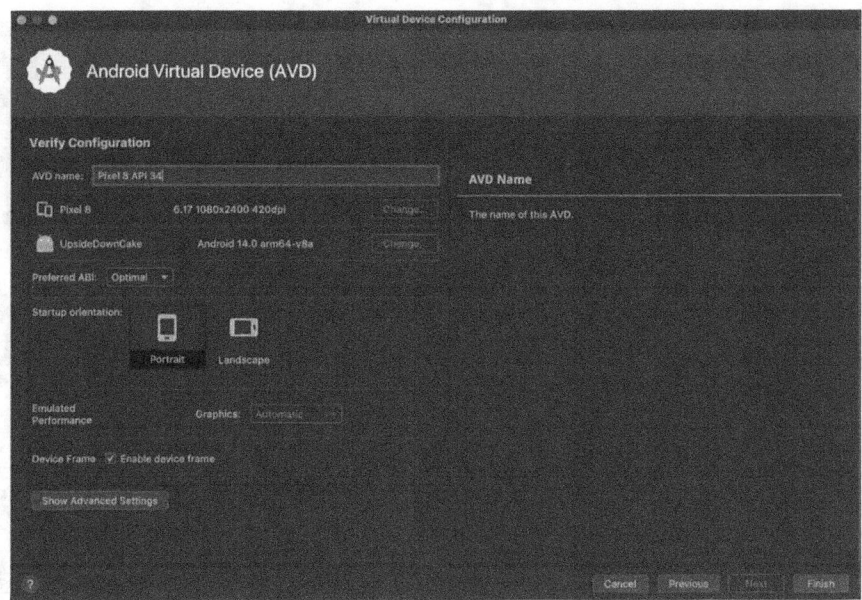

Figure 2-9. *Set Android Virtual Device Configuration*

9. Navigate back to Device Manager and you should see the emulator created.

10. Click the play icon and the emulator should be booted.

23

CHAPTER 2   GETTING STARTED WITH APPIUM 3.0

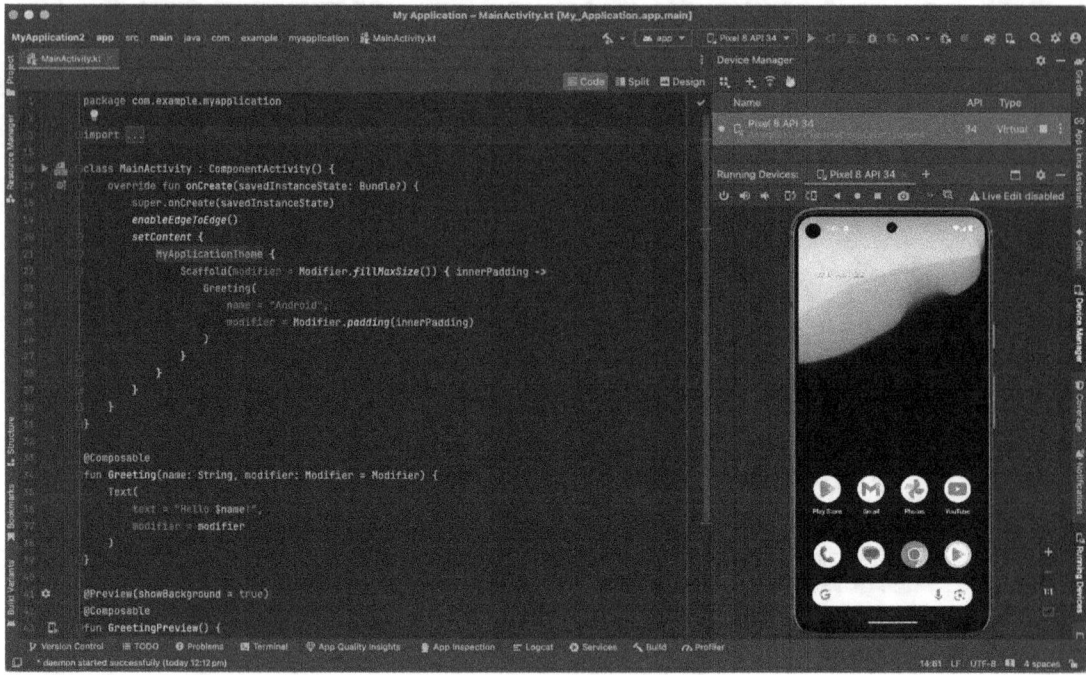

BINGO!! Android emulator is set up for our test automation.

Install Android Studio for Windows

The process of installing Android Studio and the Android emulator is largely the same for Mac and Windows, with the primary difference being how you configure environment variables. However, setting up environment variables on Windows required the below steps.

Set Up Environment Variables for Windows

1. Open System Properties

    – Right-click "This PC" or "Computer" and select "Properties."

    – Click "Advanced system settings."

    – Click the "Environment Variables" button.

2. Add `ANDROID_HOME`

    - Under "System Variables," click "New" and enter the following:
    - **Variable Name:** `ANDROID_HOME`
    - **Variable Value:** Path to your Android SDK (e.g., `C:\Users\YourUsername\AppData\Local\Android\Sdk`)

3. Add the SDK tools to the `Path` variable

    - Append the following paths to the `Path` variable:
    - `%ANDROID_HOME%\platform-tools`
    - `%ANDROID_HOME%\tools`

Set Up Environment Variables for Mac/Linux

1. Edit Shell Profile

    - Open a terminal and edit your shell profile (e.g., `.bashrc`, `.bash_profile`, or `.zshrc`)

2. Add Environment Variables

```
export ANDROID_HOME=$HOME/Library/Android/sdk
export PATH=$PATH:$ANDROID_HOME/platform-tools
export PATH=$PATH:$ANDROID_HOME/tools
```

3. Apply Changes

    - Save the file and reload the shell profile by running `source ~/.bash_profile` or `source ~/.zshrc`

Verify ANDROID_HOME

After setting up the ANDROID_HOME environment variable, it's essential to verify that it has been configured correctly. This step ensures that your development environment can correctly locate the Android SDK, which is critical for building and testing Android applications.

Why Verifying ANDROID_HOME Is Important

The ANDROID_HOME environment variable tells your system where to find the Android SDK. Appium server depends on this variable to execute commands related to Android, such as installing the application, checking for device information, and any adb commands to an emulator or a connected device. If ANDROID_HOME is not set up correctly, you may encounter issues running Appium tests on android device/emulator.

How to Verify ANDROID_HOME

1. **Open a Terminal or Command Prompt**

   - On **Windows**, you can open the command prompt by searching for "cmd" in the Start menu.

   - On **Mac/Linux**, open the terminal from your applications or by using a keyboard shortcut (Cmd + Space and typing "Terminal" on Mac).

   - For Windows, run the command echo %ANDROID_HOME%.

   - For Mac/Linux, run the command echo $ANDROID_HOME.

This command will print the current value of the `ANDROID_HOME` environment variable. It should be the path you set during the configuration setup (e.g., C:\Users\YourUsername\AppData\Local\Android\Sdk on Windows or /Users/YourUsername/Library/Android/sdk on Mac).

Working with Emulators

Now that we have successfully installed the Android emulator and booted it up, you might be eager to see your setup in action. One of the simplest ways to verify that your emulator is running correctly is by using the adb devices command. This command lists all devices connected to your development environment, including both emulators and physical devices.

When you run `adb devices` after booting your emulator, you should see it listed along with its unique identifier. This confirms that your emulator is up and running, ready to be used for testing. However, if you connect a real Android device to your computer, you might notice that it doesn't appear in the list immediately. This occurs because real devices require additional settings to be configured before they can be recognized by `adb`. We see this in the later chapters.

iOS-Specific Prerequisites

One major issue surrounding iOS automation using Appium is the **platform dependency**. Appium restricts iOS testing to macOS because real devices and simulators require different configurations. This limitation is due to technical reasons tied to the Apple ecosystem.

Apple's integrated development environment, which includes the necessary SDKs, is called **Xcode**. Xcode is essential for developers who want to develop, test, or automate iOS applications, as it is only compatible with the macOS operating system. Additionally, Xcode features an **iOS Simulator**.

The iOS Simulator in Xcode enables application developers to test applications intended for iOS-enabled devices. Essentially, the simulator acts like an actual device but is lighter and faster, making it ideal for preliminary testing. However, iOS simulators can only operate on macOS, given that they are integrated into the Xcode environment.

Install Xcode on Mac

Before installing Xcode, make sure your mac machine has enough disk space, as Xcode and its components can require at least 10–20 GB.

There are two ways to install Xcode: first, you can download it from the App Store, and second, you can download it from developer.apple.com. To do either of these, you must first create an iCloud account.

Open the App Store on your mac and search for Xcode. Click the Get or Download button. If prompted to enter your Apple ID credentials, please provide your iCloud ID. Refer to Figure 2-10.

CHAPTER 2   GETTING STARTED WITH APPIUM 3.0

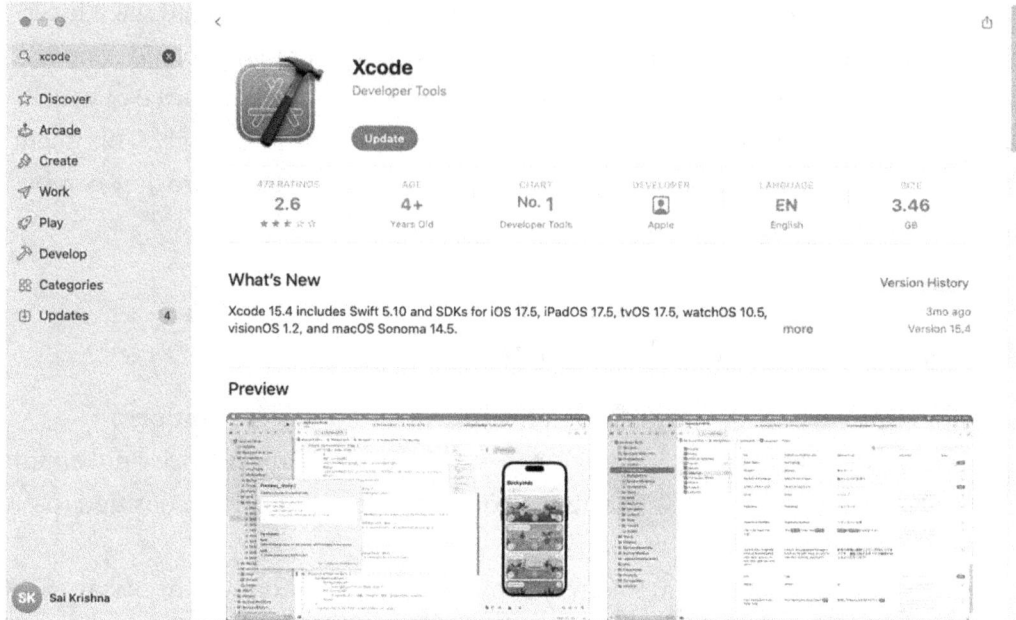

Figure 2-10. *Install Xcode from App Store*

Wait for the installation to be completed. This process will take time depending on your internet speed and system performance. Once the installation is complete, the Xcode icon will appear in your application folder and Launchpad.

Install Xcode Command-Line Tools

Xcode command-line tools is a package of development tools provided by Apple that allows you to perform software development tasks directly from the command line on macOS. You must be wondering why command-line tools are required when I have installed an entire Xcode for 10 odd GB. You will understand when we come to using real devices for test automation. For now, let's go ahead and see how to install the command-line tool.

Open the terminal and run the command as per Figure 2-11.

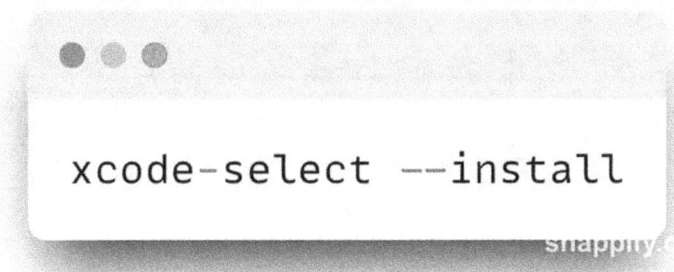

Figure 2-11. *Install Xcode command line*

Next step is we want to make sure we are able to run xcrun simctl command; this helps Appium to handle all simulator-related actions like creating a simulator, deleting, getting simulator preference, and more for your test execution. Run the below command in the terminal to make sure the simctl command is working.

```
xcrun simctl --version
@(#)PROGRAM:simctl  PROJECT:CoreSimulator-944.5
```

If you encounter an error as simctl command is not found, then follow the below steps.

Open the **Xcode** menu at the top, then select **Settings**, and then select the **Locations** tab and select a value from the command-line tools. Refer to Figure 2-12.

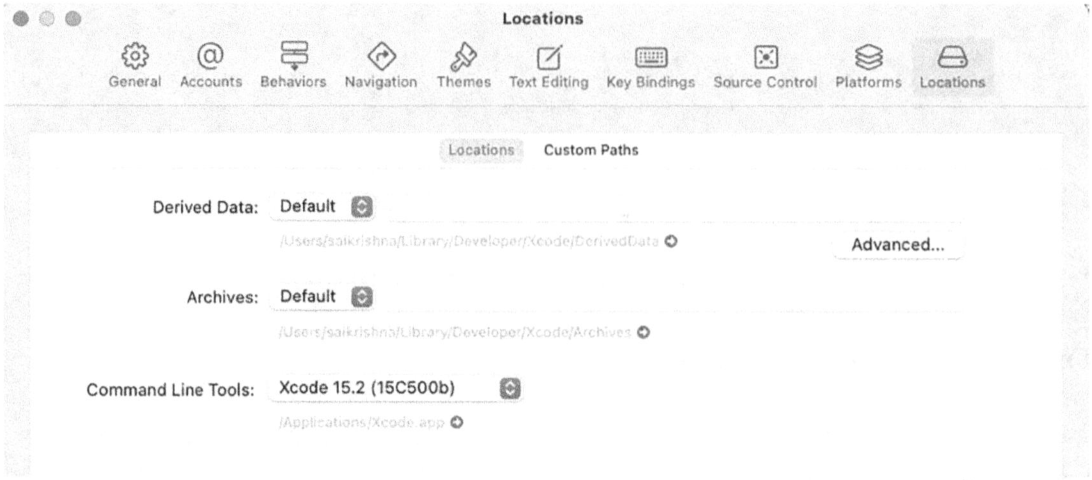

CHAPTER 2   GETTING STARTED WITH APPIUM 3.0

Figure 2-12.   Command-line tool path

BINGO! Now we have all the required software and tools setup for iOS.

Appium Driver Installation

Appium drivers are the essential components that enable Appium to automate mobile applications across various platforms like iOS and Android. Each driver acts as a bridge between the Appium server and the specific mobile platform it is designed to automate.

When you install the Appium server, it comes as a bare-bones installation with no drivers included. This means that by default, Appium cannot automate any mobile applications until the appropriate driver is installed. The choice of driver depends entirely on the platform and the type of application you want to automate:

- **iOS Automation:** If you are automating iOS applications, you'll need to install the XCUITest driver.

- **Android Automation:** For Android applications, the UIAutomator2 driver is required.

Listing Supported Drivers

Appium officially supports multiple drivers, each designed to automate different platforms. You can list all the drivers supported by Appium. Refer to Figure 2-13.

CHAPTER 2   GETTING STARTED WITH APPIUM 3.0

Open the terminal and run the below command.

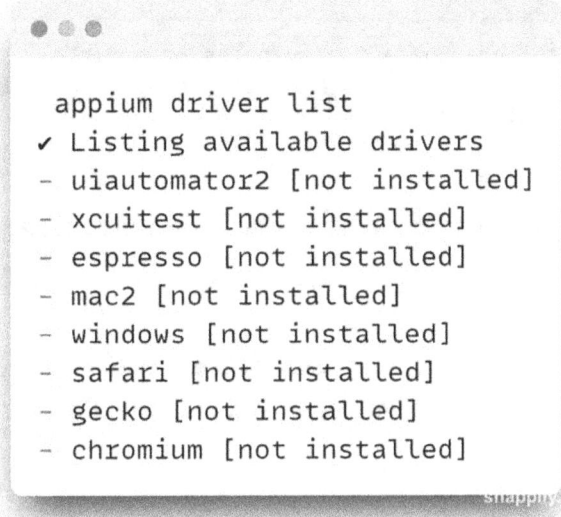

Figure 2-13. *List of drivers supported by Appium*

The command **appium driver list** returned a list of available drivers, including their installation status.

Install Drivers

Appium 2.0 allows you to install multiple drivers which can be updated independently and removed as well. To install a specific driver, use the command **appium driver install** followed by the driver name. There are multiple ways a driver can be installed.

1. Installing Drivers Maintained by Appium Dev Team

Let's walk through the process of installing a driver that is maintained and managed by the official Appium dev team. We'll focus on installing the **XCUITest driver** as an example, but the same steps can be applied to other drivers.

For example, to install the XCUITest driver for iOS, refer to Figure 2-14.

CHAPTER 2   GETTING STARTED WITH APPIUM 3.0

```
> appium driver install xcuitest
✓ Checking if 'appium-xcuitest-driver' is compatible
✓ Installing 'xcuitest' using NPM install spec 'appium-xcuitest-driver'
ℹ Driver xcuitest@7.24.15 successfully installed
- automationName: XCUITest
- platformNames: ["iOS","tvOS"]
```

Figure 2-14. *Installing XCUITest driver*

Now when we run the command **appium driver list**, you should see the XCUITest driver as installed and the specific version as well. Refer to Figure 2-15.

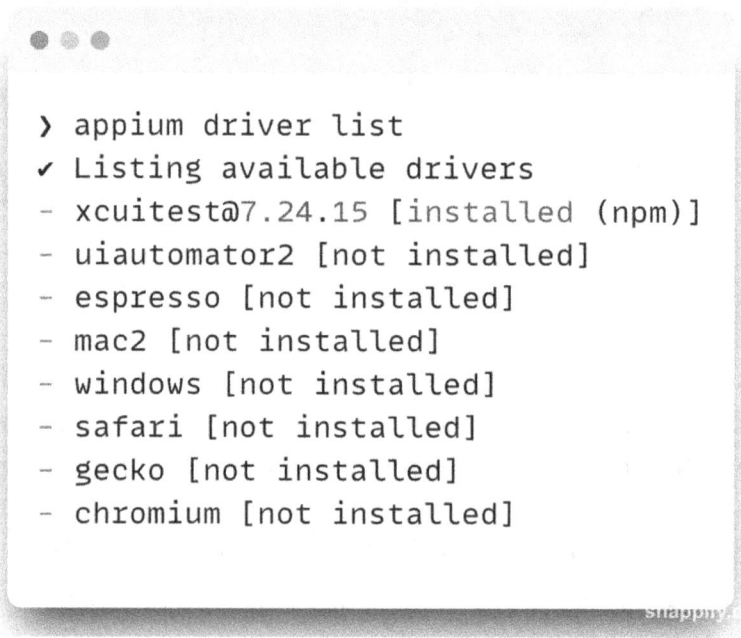

Figure 2-15. *Installed driver list*

2. Installing Drivers Maintained by Community

Let's walk through the process of installing a driver that is maintained and managed by the community. We'll focus on installing the **flutter integration driver** as an example, but the same steps can be applied to other drivers.

CHAPTER 2 GETTING STARTED WITH APPIUM 3.0

First, you need to know what are the community-maintained drivers. You can find them listed under appium.io (https://appium.io/docs/en/latest/ecosystem/drivers/#other-drivers).

Other Drivers

These drivers are not maintained by the Appium team and can be used to target additional platforms:

Driver	Installation Key	Platform(s)	Mode(s)	Supported By
Flutter	--source=npm appium-flutter-driver	iOS, Android	Native	Community
Flutter Integration	--source=npm appium-flutter-integration-driver	iOS, Android	Native	Community / @AppiumTestDistribution
LG WebOS	--source=npm appium-lg-webos-driver	LG TV	Web	HeadSpin
Linux	--source=npm @stdspa/appium-linux-driver	Linux	Native	@fantonglang
Roku	--source=npm @headspinio/appium-roku-driver	Roku	Native	HeadSpin
Tizen	--source=npm appium-tizen-driver	Android	Native	Community / Samsung
TizenTV	--source=npm appium-tizen-tv-driver	Samsung TV	Web	HeadSpin
Youi	--source=npm appium-youiengine-driver	iOS, Android, macOS, Linux, tvOS	Native	Community / You.i

Open the terminal and run the below command.

appium driver install --source npm appium-flutter-integration-driver

```
> appium driver install --source npm appium-flutter-integration-driver

✓ Checking if 'appium-flutter-integration-driver' is compatible
✓ Installing 'appium-flutter-integration-driver'
ℹ Driver flutter-integration@1.1.3 successfully installed
  - automationName: FlutterIntegration
  - platformNames: ["Android","iOS"]
```

Now when we run the command **appium driver list**, you should see the flutter integration driver as installed and the specific version as well. Refer to Figure 2-16.

```
> appium driver list
✓ Listing available drivers
        - xcuitest@7.24.15 [installed (npm)]
        - flutter-integration@1.1.3 [installed (npm)]
        - uiautomator2 [not installed]
        - espresso [not installed]
        - mac2 [not installed]
        - windows [not installed]
        - safari [not installed]
        - gecko [not installed]
        - chromium [not installed]
```

Figure 2-16. Installed driver list

3. Install and Test a Driver Locally

Now, imagine a situation where you have identified a bug in one of the drivers perhaps that you frequently use or even a community-maintained driver. Before submitting a fix to the respective driver repository, it's important to test your changes locally to ensure they work fine without introducing new issues. But how do you install and test the modified version of a driver on your local machine? Let's explore the steps involved in installing a driver locally.

1. Clone the driver from the GitHub repository provided its open source. Run the command

```
git clone https://github.com/AppiumTestDistribution/appium-flutter-integration-driver
```

2. Build the driver based on their approach, and this will vary for different projects. In the case of flutter-integration-driver, first you need to install all the dependencies and build the code for local use.

CHAPTER 2   GETTING STARTED WITH APPIUM 3.0

```
npm install && npm run bundle
```

3. Now as the driver is all set up locally, you need to make sure Appium is aware of this driver for which we need to run the install command where the source is set to local with the path of the built repository.

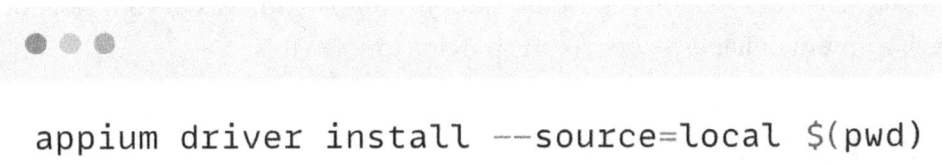

```
appium driver install --source=local $(pwd)
```

Now when we run the command **appium driver list**, you should see the flutter integration driver as installed and also mention that it's in dev mode because it's not installed from repo source. Refer to Figure 2-17.

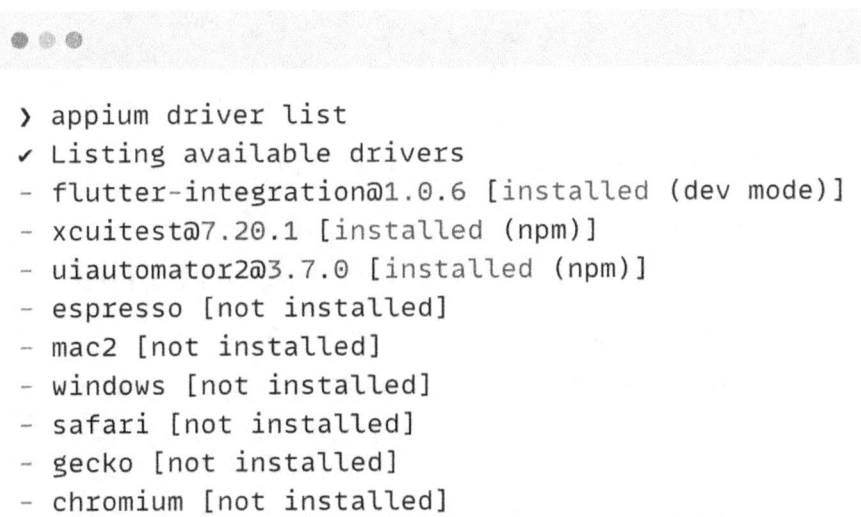

```
> appium driver list
✓ Listing available drivers
  - flutter-integration@1.0.6 [installed (dev mode)]
  - xcuitest@7.20.1 [installed (npm)]
  - uiautomator2@3.7.0 [installed (npm)]
  - espresso [not installed]
  - mac2 [not installed]
  - windows [not installed]
  - safari [not installed]
  - gecko [not installed]
  - chromium [not installed]
```

Figure 2-17. Installed driver list in dev mode

35

CHAPTER 2   GETTING STARTED WITH APPIUM 3.0

Appium Plugin Installation

The Appium plugins that extend the regular features of Appium makes it possible for you to modify and improve your Appium server capabilities. When it comes to plugins, they can either alter how sessions are processed, register a new command, or overload the existing one. Just as drivers do, there are plugins officially and communally maintained which can be installed, updated, or removed without affecting the Appium server.

When you install the Appium server, it comes as a bare-bones installation with no plugins included. This means that by default, Appium does not have active plugins. The choice of plugin depends entirely on what is the use case that you want to handle.

Let's take a use case where you would want to compare images in your test code. Let's see if Appium officially supports any plugins to solve this.

Listing Supported Plugins

Appium officially supports multiple plugins, each designed to solve different problems. You can list all the plugins supported by Appium.

Open the terminal and run the command **appium plugin list**.

```
> appium plugin list
✔ Listing available plugins
- images [not installed]
- execute-driver [not installed]
- relaxed-caps [not installed]
- universal-xml [not installed]
```

The command **appium plugin list** returned a list of available plugins, including their installation status.

CHAPTER 2   GETTING STARTED WITH APPIUM 3.0

Install Plugins

Appium 3.0 allows you to install multiple plugins which can be updated independently and removed as well. To install a specific driver, use the command **appium plugin install** followed by the plugin name. There are multiple ways a plugin can be installed.

1. Installing Plugins Maintained by Appium Dev Team

Let's walk through the process of installing a plugin that is maintained and managed by the official Appium dev team. We'll focus on installing the **images plugin** as an example, but the same steps can be applied to other plugins.

```
> appium plugin install images
✓ Checking if '@appium/images-plugin' is compatible
✓ Installing 'images' using NPM install spec '@appium/images-plugin'
i Plugin images@3.0.18 successfully installed
```

Now when we run the command **appium plugin list**, you should see the images plugin as installed and the specific version as well. Refer to Figure 2-18.

```
> appium plugin list
✓ Listing available plugins
- images@3.0.18 [installed (npm)]
- execute-driver [not installed]
- relaxed-caps [not installed]
- universal-xml [not installed]
```

Figure 2-18. Installed plugin list from NPM maintained by Appium team

CHAPTER 2   GETTING STARTED WITH APPIUM 3.0

2. Installing Plugins Maintained by Community

Let's walk through the process of installing a plugin that is maintained and managed by the community. We'll focus on installing the **Appium Device Farm plugin** as an example, but the same steps can be applied to other plugins.

First you need to know what are the community-maintained plugins. You can find them listed under appium.io (`https://appium.io/docs/en/latest/ecosystem/plugins`).

Other Plugins

These plugins are not maintained by the Appium team and can provide additional functionality:

Plugin	Installation Key	Description	Supported By
AltUnity	`--source=npm appium-altunity-plugin`	Target Unity games and apps for automation with a new context, via the AltUnityTester framework	HeadSpin
Device Farm	`--source=npm appium-device-farm`	Manage and create driver sessions on connected Android devices and iOS simulators	@AppiumTestDistribution
Gestures	`--source=npm appium-gestures-plugin`	Perform basic gestures using W3C Actions	@AppiumTestDistribution
Interceptor	`--source=npm appium-interceptor`	Intercept and mock API requests and responses	@AppiumTestDistribution
OCR	`--source=npm appium-ocr-plugin`	Find elements via OCR text	@jlipps
Reporter	`--source=npm appium-reporter-plugin`	Generate standalone consolidated HTML reports with screenshots	@AppiumTestDistribution
Wait	`--source=npm appium-wait-plugin`	Manage global element wait timeouts	@AppiumTestDistribution

Open the terminal and run the below command.

```
appium driver install --source npm appium-device-farm
```

CHAPTER 2　GETTING STARTED WITH APPIUM 3.0

```
> appium plugin install --source npm appium-device-farm

✓ Checking if 'appium-device-farm' is compatible
✓ Installing 'appium-device-farm'
ⅰ Plugin device-farm@9.2.11 successfully installed
```

Figure 2-19. *Installed plugin list from NPM maintaned by Community*

3. Install and Test a Plugin Locally

Now, imagine a situation where you have identified a bug in one of the plugins–perhaps that you frequently use or even a community-maintained plugin. Before submitting a fix to the respective plugin repository, it's important to test your changes locally to ensure they work fine without introducing new issues. But how do you install and test the modified version of a plugin on your local machine? Let's explore the steps involved in installing a plugin locally.

1. Clone the driver from the GitHub repository provided its open source. Run the command

```
git clone https://github.com/AppiumTestDistribution/appium-device-farm
```

2. Build the plugin based on their approach, and this will vary for different projects. In the case of appium-device-farm, first you need to install all the dependencies and build the code for local use.

CHAPTER 2   GETTING STARTED WITH APPIUM 3.0

Now as the plugin is all set up locally, you need to make sure Appium is aware of this plugin for which we need to run the install command where the source is set to local with the path of the built repository.

```
appium plugin install --source=local $(pwd)
```

Now when we run the command **appium plugin list**, you should see the Appium Device Farm plugin as installed and also mention that it's in dev mode because it's not installed from repo source.

```
> appium plugin list
✓ Listing available plugins
- device-farm@9.2.11 [installed (dev mode)]
- images [not installed]
- execute-driver [not installed]
- relaxed-caps [not installed]
- universal-xml [not installed]
```

Appium Doctor

When working with Appium, setting up your environment correctly is crucial. This is where Appium Doctor comes into play. Appium Doctor is a command-line utility that verifies the configuration of your environment, ensuring that all the necessary tools and dependencies for Appium are installed and properly set up. This tool is especially useful for quickly identifying and resolving common setup issues.

Why Use Appium Doctor?

In the above sections, we have seen the process of setting up a mobile automation environment and its complex, with various tools like Java, Android SDK, Node.js, and Xcode needing to be correctly installed and configured. Even a small misconfiguration can lead to hours of frustration when trying to run your tests. Appium Doctor simplifies this process by automatically checking for these dependencies and alerting you to any issues.

Using Appium Doctor helps

Save Time: Instead of manually verifying each component of your setup, Appium Doctor provides a quick overview, pinpointing any problems.

Reduce Errors: By ensuring that all required tools are installed and correctly configured, Appium Doctor reduces the likelihood of environment-related errors during test execution.

Ease Troubleshooting: When something does go wrong, Appium Doctor's output can guide you in identifying and fixing the issue, speeding up the troubleshooting process.

How Appium Doctor Works

Appium Doctor performs a series of checks based on the drivers or plugin you're working with. For example:

> **Android**: It checks if adb (Android Debug Bridge) is installed, if the Android SDK is properly set up, and if the Java Development Kit (JDK) is accessible.

> **iOS**: It verifies that Xcode is installed, checks for the presence of ffmpeg, and more.

Run the command in your terminal **`appium driver doctor xcuitest`**.

```
> appium driver doctor xcuitest
Running 6 doctor checks for the "xcuitest" driver
info Doctor ### Starting doctor diagnostics ###
info Doctor ✔ HOME is set to: /Users/saikrishna
info Doctor ✔ xCode is installed at '/Applications/Xcode.app/Contents/Developer'
info Doctor ✔ xCode tools are installed and work properly
info Doctor ✔ applesimutils is installed at: /opt/homebrew/bin/applesimutils
info Doctor ✔ ffmpeg exists at '/opt/homebrew/bin/ffmpeg'
info Doctor ✔ idb and idb_companion are installed
info Doctor ### Diagnostic completed, 0 required fixes needed, 0 optional fixes possible. ###
info Doctor
info Doctor Everything looks good, bye!
info Doctor
```

This command runs a series of checks and displays the results in the terminal. If any issues are found, Appium Doctor provides detailed messages explaining what needs to be fixed.

Summary

In this chapter, we covered the essential prerequisites for setting up Appium, focusing on the requirements for both Android and iOS platforms. We began by outlining the general prerequisites, such as installing Node.js, which is the foundation for running Appium, and setting up the Java Development Kit (JDK) necessary for Android testing. We then delved into Android-specific prerequisites, including the installation of the Android SDK and the configuration of environment variables, ensuring your system is ready for testing on both emulators and real devices. The chapter also discussed iOS-specific prerequisites, emphasizing the need for a macOS environment, installing Xcode, and configuring Xcode command-line tools to facilitate iOS testing. Additionally, we explored the installation and verification processes for both Android and iOS, guiding you through setting up a functional testing environment. Finally, the chapter introduced Appium's driver and plugin installations, explaining how to extend Appium's capabilities for automating mobile applications across various platforms. By following the steps outlined, you should now be equipped with a solid foundation to begin mobile test automation using Appium.

CHAPTER 3

Real Device Configuration

Module Introduction

Earlier in this guide, we gave very detailed guidance on how to configure the necessary software for both Android and iOS platforms. This basis setting up involved installing development tools as well as SDKs including any dependencies that are required for building and testing mobile applications. Furthermore, not only did we set up software, we also looked into the emulator-based virtual device creation process specific for Android OS.

Although emulators are useful tools during the initial testing phase or debugging stage, there exist some shortcomings in their use. For example, they may not reflect actual device performance closely especially for things like hardware-specific functions or battery life sensor accuracy, among others. Also, various features found in some devices like camera and fingerprint, among others, do not function similarly probably due to lack of complete support in some cases on emulators.

As you will approach the app launch to Play Store and App Store, testing it on real devices becomes necessary to see how it behaves across different hardware and software configurations present today. Real device testing will help you identify problems that might remain invisible when using emulators, hence improving accuracy over possible behavior by end users before shipping off anything.

What You Will Learn

In this chapter, we will guide you through the process of configuring your environment to run tests on real Android and iOS devices. Testing on real devices allows you to gain insights into how your application performs in real-world scenarios, including how it handles different hardware configurations, operating system versions, and network conditions.

We'll start by setting up Android real devices, covering everything from enabling developer options on the device to configuring Appium to recognize and interact with your Android phone or tablet. Afterward, we'll move on to setting up iOS real devices, which involves additional steps like obtaining the necessary permissions and certificates to communicate with the device.

By the end of this chapter, you'll be equipped to run your automated tests on actual hardware, ensuring that your application is fully optimized and ready for release on real devices.

Let's dive into the setup process, starting with Android real devices.

Setup Android Real Device

For efficient testing of your Android applications on an actual gadget, the device has to be configured in such a way that it can be recognized by the Android Debug Bridge (ADB) which is a vital tool for communication between your development environment and the device. This way, not just USB debugging but connection of the device over Wi-Fi is made possible, hence making it more flexible and convenient particularly when physical connections are not practical.

For ADB recognition and stable connection over a wireless network, there are some critical changes that should be done on the Android device.

Making the real device visible with the Android Debug Bridge, you need to first turn on the USB debugging feature in the testing device.

Steps to enable USB debugging on an android device:

1. **Unlock Developer Options** (if not already enabled)

    - Go to **Settings ➤ About Phone**.

    - Scroll down and find **Build Number**.

    - Tap on **Build Number 7 times** until you see a message that says "You are now a developer!" (or something similar).

2. **Enable USB Debugging**

    - Go back to **Settings**.

    - Now, you should see **Developer Options** under **System** (or just in the main menu on some devices).

- Enter **Developer Options**, and scroll down to find **USB Debugging**.
- Toggle it on, and confirm the action.

3. **Connect Your Device to Your Computer**
   - Use a USB cable to connect the device to your computer.
   - Once connected, you may see a pop-up on the device asking if you want to allow USB debugging from this computer. Click **Allow**.

4. **Verify the Connection**

   Open a terminal or command prompt on your computer and type:

   adb devices

Your device should appear in the list with its serial number if indeed the connection was successful.

You will therefore be able to use any ADB command on the device at this juncture. For battery information retrieval, the following command can be of use:

adb shell dumpsys battery

It is also possible to attach multiple android devices to one computer. All the serial numbers of the connected devices are shown once you execute the adb devices command in the terminal. If you want to execute an ADB command for a specific device, then you have to provide its serial number as follows:

adb -s serialno shell dumpsys battery

To wrap up the Android setup, you're now equipped with the essential tools and commands to interact with your Android devices through ADB. With this foundation in place, let's move on to setting up and working with iOS devices.

Setup iOS Real Device

To run your Appium iOS tests on a real device, there are a few essential steps you need to take beforehand. First, make sure that your device is trusted by the system. Here's how you can do that: Start by opening the Xcode on your computer; once the Xcode

CHAPTER 3   REAL DEVICE CONFIGURATION

is opened, connect the real iOS device. When the device is connected, at this point a pop up will appear on your device to trust it. Make sure to accept the prompt (refer to Figure 3-1) as it's crucial for ensuring that your device is properly trusted. This step is necessary to prepare your device for testing with Appium.

Figure 3-1. *Trust device to Xcode*

Next step is we need to enable developer mode that is hidden inside the settings app on your device. Navigate to `Settings > Privacy & Security > Developer mode and turn on the mode.`

CHAPTER 3   REAL DEVICE CONFIGURATION

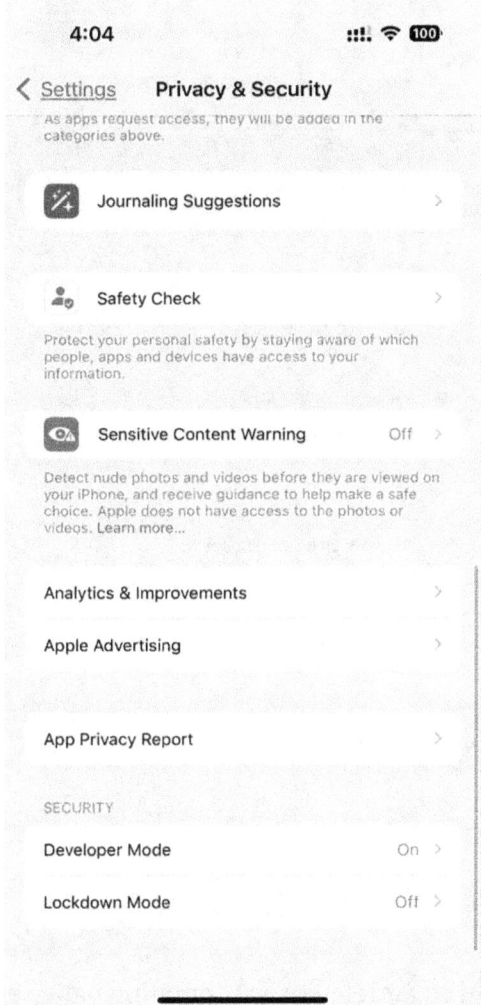

Once this is completed, the device needs to be restarted. Once the device is booted and developer mode is turned on, go to the settings application and search for **Developer** section and then enable UI automation. This setting is important because it allows your tests to interact with UI elements on your real device. By enabling this, you ensure that your tests can run smoothly.

CHAPTER 3   REAL DEVICE CONFIGURATION

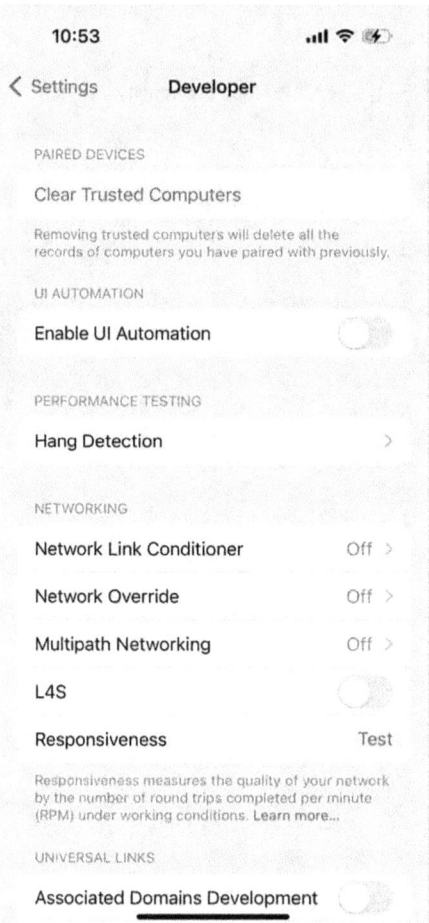

Everything we covered so far relates to automating native applications. When you have a situation to automate mobile WebViews within the app or want to use Safari browser on your device, you need to enable another toggle.

`Settings > Safari > Advanced`

Now toggle on remote automation. This enables for WebView automation.

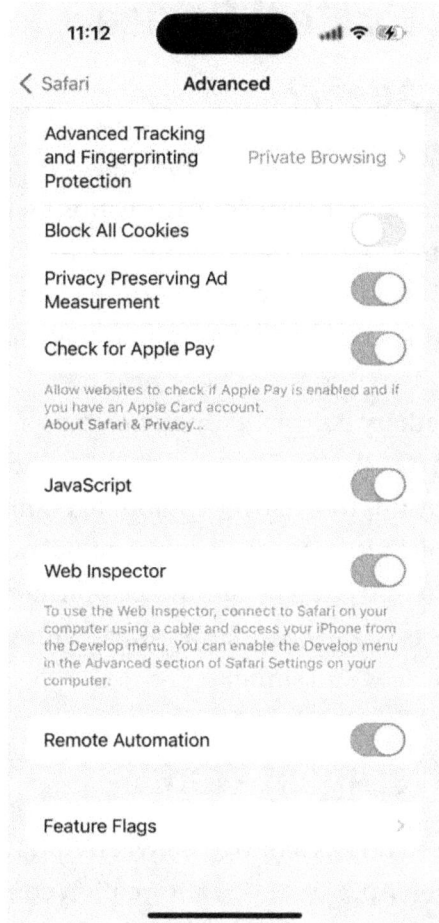

With these steps completed, we have set up most of the necessary components required for automating tests on iOS real devices. Key configurations like device pairing, Appium settings, and other essential prerequisites are now in place. However, the final step, which involves setting up the provisioning profile, remains. Once the provisioning profile is configured, the iOS real device will be fully ready for seamless test automation, allowing you to execute test scripts with precision on actual hardware.

CHAPTER 3 REAL DEVICE CONFIGURATION

WebDriverAgent for Real Device

What Is WebDriverAgent?

WebDriverAgent (WDA) is essentially a server that operates on actual iOS devices, enabling Appium to simulate user interactions with apps on them. Initially, the main goal of creating this program was automated testing mobile applications iOS devices by Facebook. At some point, Facebook ceased supporting it; however, Appium team started using their forked repository, hence ensuring continued support under the umbrella of Appium.

WDA acts as an intermediary between Appium client's automation commands and real actions executed on an iOS app. It allows users to interact with UI elements such as swiping or tapping. This way this tool allows Appium to communicate with the app and send commands to it as though it were driven by an actual person.

Importantly, WDA is not only used to automate applications on iPhones or iPads—its functionality also supports tvOS. It is an important feature as it allows for automated testing on both real tvOS devices and simulators.

How Does WebDriverAgent Work?

WebDriverAgent works like acting as a bridge between Appium and the iOS device or tvOS device under test. When Appium sends automation commands such as tapping a button or scrolling a screen, WDA translated these commands into native iOS interactions and executed them on the device. These commands don't go directly to WDA; instead, they first pass through appium-xcuitest-driver.

The appium-xcuitest-driver sits between the Appium server and WDA. WDA receives a request from the appium-xcuitest-driver and performs tasks based on the request like find UI elements, scrolling elements, executing gestures, and verifying app states. This setup allows for precise simulation of real user interactions. Once the actions are performed, WDA communicates back to the appium-xcuitest-driver module which in turn relays the information to Appium. This multilayer communication ensures that Appium can effectively manage and control the application under test on the device.

CHAPTER 3 REAL DEVICE CONFIGURATION

How to Build WebDriverAgent?

Appium XCUITest driver takes care of building and installation of WDA on simulators as they don't require any signing certificate using Xcode's command-line utility xcodebuild. Unlike simulators, to install WDA on real devices, you must have a valid provisioning profile, which includes signing the app and linking it to a development team.

If you have a personal Apple ID, then the provision profile generated with this account will only last for six days, meaning WDA build for real devices using this profile will not work after six days from the day of generation.

If you want to register for a development account, then you need to pay $100 USD to Apple (https://developer.apple.com/).

Next step is we need to open the WDA in the Xcode application. Appium XCUITest driver comes with the appium-webdriveragent project.

Run the command `appium driver run xcuitest open-wda`.

This should open the WebDriverAgent in Xcode. Select Automatically manage signing and add Bundle Identifier value; in this case, I have changed the default value to com.appium.book.2024.

Xcode will automatically sync this profile, and it should be available for app signing.

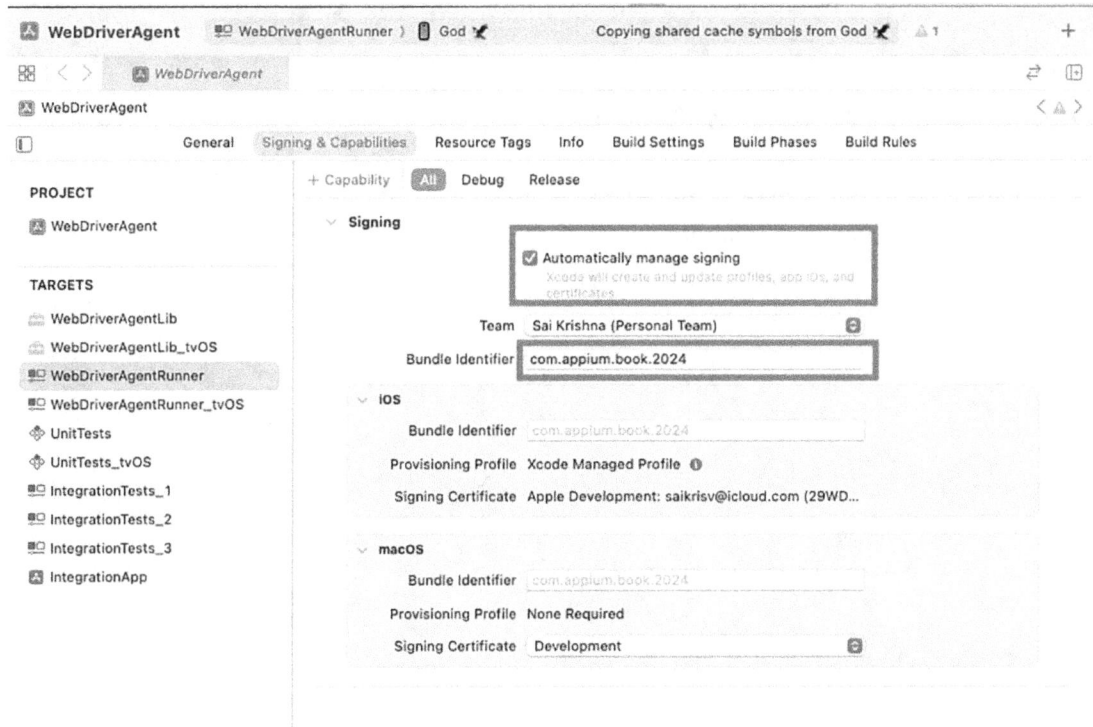

Connect your real device and wait for it to complete indexing. Once your device is found by Xcode, select `Product > Test`.

WebDriverAgent should be installed on your device, and Xcode should throw an error failed to open as this should be trusted on the device. Refer to Figure 3-2.

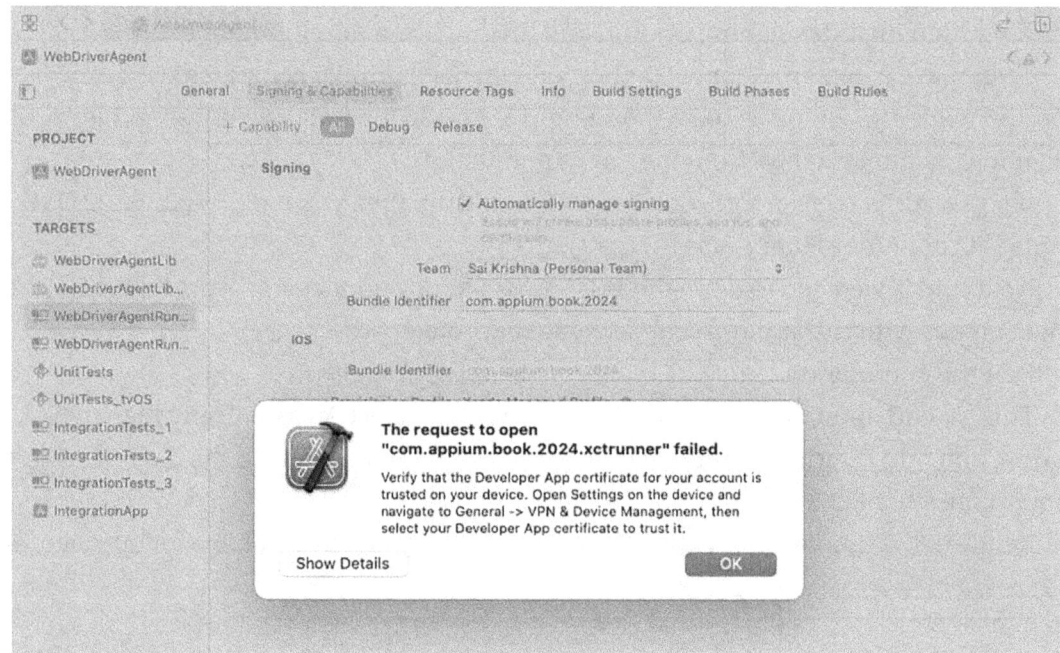

Figure 3-2. *Trust the Developer certificate*

As mentioned in the error pop-up, navigate General ➤ Device Management and trust the WDA application installed.

CHAPTER 3   REAL DEVICE CONFIGURATION

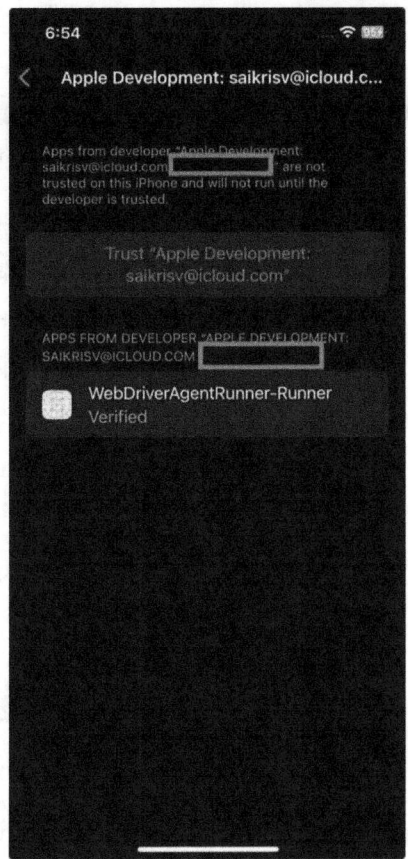

After trusting the application, you should be able to launch the WDA on a real device and should see an "Automation Running" message in the device.

When integrating WebDriverAgent (WDA) with your test automation setup, many of the foundational elements may seem straightforward at first glance. However, the key step in making this integration truly seamless is creating an IPA (iOS app) of the WebDriverAgent. This is not as simple as creating an IPA for a regular iOS application, as WebDriverAgent is not a conventional application, but rather a **testing framework**.

By packaging WDA into an IPA, you can easily deploy it to any iOS device as part of your CI/CD pipeline or local testing setup, which eliminates the need to manually build and deploy it each time you run tests.

CHAPTER 3 REAL DEVICE CONFIGURATION

Steps to Create a WebDriverAgent IPA

1. Navigate to the path /Users/username/.appium/node_modules/appium-xcuitest-driver/node_modules/appium-webdriveragent/

2. Run the command

   ```
   $ xcodebuild clean build-for-testing -project WebDriverAgent.xcodeproj -derivedDataPath appium_wda_ios -scheme WebDriverAgentRunner -destination generic/platform=iOS CODE_SIGNING_ALLOWED=NO
   ```

3. Navigate to /Users/XXX/Library/Developer/Xcode/DerivedData/WebDriverAgent-thiswillchane/Build/Products/Debug-iphoneos/

4. Create a folder Payload and paste the WebDriverAgentRunner-Runner.app

5. Right-click the WebDriverAgentRunner-Runner.app; select show contents and remove all the files under framework

6. Repack the Payload as ipa (zip and then rename to wda.ipa)

7. Next and final step to codesign (https://developer.apple.com/documentation/xcode/using-the-latest-code-signature-format) the wda.ipa

Executing these steps for every build and also in the CI/CD is not an easy task. All these can be executed with the below script which also solves the entire building and codesiging WebDriverAgent for generic devices.

```
import { exec } from 'child_process';
import path from 'path';
import util from 'util';
import fs from 'fs';
// eslint-disable-next-line @typescript-eslint/ban-ts-comment
// @ts-ignore
import Applesign from 'applesign';
import archiver from 'archiver';
import yargs from 'yargs/yargs';
```

```
import { hideBin } from 'yargs/helpers';
import Listr, { ListrContext } from 'listr';
import { provision } from 'ios-mobileprovision-finder';
import os from 'os';
import { Observable, Subscriber } from 'rxjs';
// eslint-disable-next-line @typescript-eslint/ban-ts-comment
// @ts-ignore
import { select } from '@inquirer/prompts';

const execAsync = util.promisify(exec);
const WDA_BUILD_PATH = '/appium_wda_ios/Build/Products/Debug-iphoneos';
const PROVISION_FILE_PATH_PREFIX = path.join(
  os.homedir(),
  'Library/MobileDevice/Provisioning Profiles',
);

type Context = ListrContext & CliOptions;

interface CliOptions {
  mobileProvisioningFile?: string;
  wdaProjectPath?: string;
}

const getOptions = async () => {
  const argv: CliOptions = await yargs(hideBin(process.argv)).options({
    'mobile-provisioning-file': {
      desc: 'Path to the mobile provisioning file which is used to sign the
      webdriver agent',
      type: 'string',
    },
    'wda-project-path': {
      desc: 'Path to webdriver agent xcode project',
      type: 'string',
    },
  }).argv;

  return {
```

```
      mobileProvisioningFile: argv.mobileProvisioningFile,
      wdaProjectPath: argv.wdaProjectPath,
    };
  };
};
const getMobileProvisioningFile = async (mobileProvisioningFile?:
string) => {
  if (mobileProvisioningFile) {
    if (!fs.existsSync(mobileProvisioningFile) || !fs.statSync(mobile
    ProvisioningFile).isFile()) {
      throw new Error(`Mobile provisioning file ${mobileProvisioningFile}
      does not exists`);
    }
    return mobileProvisioningFile;
  } else {
    const provisioningFiles = provision.read();
    if (!provisioningFiles || !provisioningFiles.length) {
      throw new Error('No mobileprovision file found on the machine');
    }
    const prompt = await select({
      message: 'Select the mobileprovision to use for signing',
      choices: provisioningFiles.map((file) => ({
        value: file.UUID,
        name: `${file.Name.split(':')[1] || file.Name} (Team: ${file.
        TeamName}) (${file.UUID})`,
      })),
    });

    return path.join(PROVISION_FILE_PATH_PREFIX, `${prompt}.
    mobileprovision`);
  }
};
const getWdaProject = async (wdaProjectPath?: string) => {
  if (wdaProjectPath) {
    if (!fs.existsSync(wdaProjectPath) || !fs.statSync(wdaProjectPath).
    isDirectory()) {
```

```
      throw new Error(`Unable to find webdriver agent project in path
        ${wdaProjectPath}`);
    }
    return wdaProjectPath;
  }

  try {
    const { stdout } = await execAsync('find $HOME/.appium -name
    WebDriverAgent.xcodeproj');
    return path.dirname(stdout.trim());
  } catch (err) {
    throw new Error('Unable to find WebDriverAgent project');
  }
};

/* Task defininitions */
async function buildWebDriverAgent(projectDir: string, logger: any) {
  try {
    const buildCommand =
      'xcodebuild clean build-for-testing -project WebDriverAgent.xcodeproj
      -derivedDataPath appium_wda_ios -scheme WebDriverAgentRunner
      -destination generic/platform=iOS CODE_SIGNING_ALLOWED=NO';
    logger(buildCommand);
    await execAsync(buildCommand, { cwd: projectDir, maxBuffer:
    undefined });
    return `${projectDir}/${WDA_BUILD_PATH}/WebDriverAgentRunner-
    Runner.app`;
  } catch (error) {
    throw new Error(`✗ Error building WebDriverAgent: ${(error as any)?.
    message}`);
  }
}

async function zipPayloadDirectory(
  outputZipPath: any,
  folderPath: any,
  observer: Subscriber<string>,
```

CHAPTER 3   REAL DEVICE CONFIGURATION

```
) {
  return new Promise<void>((resolve, reject) => {
    const output = fs.createWriteStream(outputZipPath);
    const archive = archiver('zip', { zlib: { level: 9 } });

    output.on('close', () => {
      observer.next(`Zipped ${archive.pointer()} total bytes`);
      observer.next(`Archive has been written to ${outputZipPath}`);
      resolve();
    });

    archive.on('error', (err) => {
      reject(err);
    });

    archive.pipe(output);
    archive.directory(folderPath, 'Payload');
    archive.finalize();
  });
}

(async () => {
  const cliOptions = await getOptions();
  const mobileProvisioningFile = await getMobileProvisioningFile(cliOptions.
  mobileProvisioningFile);

  const tasks = new Listr(
    [
      {
        title: '🔍 Searching for WebDriverAgent.xcodeproj',
        task: async (context: Context, task) => {
          context.wdaProjectPath = await getWdaProject(cliOptions.
          wdaProjectPath);
          task.title = `Found WebDriverAgent.xcodeproj at: ${context.
          wdaProjectPath}`;
        },
      },
```

```
{
  title: '🏗️ Building WebDriverAgent',
  task: (context: Context, task) => {
    return new Observable((observer) => {
      buildWebDriverAgent(context.wdaProjectPath, observer.next.
      bind(observer)).then(
        (wdaAppPath) => {
          context.wdaAppPath = wdaAppPath;
          task.title = 'Successfully built WebDriverAgent';
          observer.complete();
        },
      );
    });
  },
},
{
  title: 'Preparing webdrivergaent ipa',
  task: (context) => {
    return new Observable((observer) => {
      const wdaBuildPath = path.join(context.wdaProjectPath, WDA_
      BUILD_PATH);
      const payloadDirectory = path.join(wdaBuildPath, 'Payload');
      observer.next('Removing framework directory');
      fs.readdirSync(`${context.wdaAppPath}/Frameworks`).
      forEach((f) =>
        fs.rmSync(`${context.wdaAppPath}/Frameworks/${f}`, {
        recursive: true }),
      );

      observer.next('Creating Payload directory');
      execAsync(`mkdir -p ${payloadDirectory}`)
        .then(() => {
          observer.next('Payload directory created successfully');
        })
        .then(() => {
          observer.next('📦 Moving .app file to Payload
          directory...');
```

CHAPTER 3   REAL DEVICE CONFIGURATION

```
                return execAsync(`mv ${context.wdaAppPath}
                ${payloadDirectory}`);
              })
              .then(() => {
                observer.next('Packing Payload directory...');
                return zipPayloadDirectory(
                  `${wdaBuildPath}/wda-resign.zip`,
                  payloadDirectory,
                  observer,
                );
              })
              .then(() => observer.complete());
          });
        },
      },
      {
        title: 'Signing WebDriverAgent ipa',
        task: async (context, task) => {
          const wdaBuildPath = path.join(context.wdaProjectPath,
          WDA_BUILD_PATH);
          const ipaPath = `${wdaBuildPath}/wda-resign.ipa`;
          const as = new Applesign({
            mobileprovision: mobileProvisioningFile,
            outfile: ipaPath,
          });
          await as.signIPA(path.join(wdaBuildPath, 'wda-resign.zip'));
          task.title = `Successfully signed WebDriverAgent
          file ${ipaPath}`;
        },
      },
    ],
    { exitOnError: true },
  );
  await tasks.run();
})();
```

The above code will pick all the provision profiles from the mac system and also build the WDA and resign the IPA which is ready to be installed on a real device.

Summary

In this chapter, we explored the process of configuring real devices for mobile automation. We started with the setup for Android devices covering all necessary tools. We then moved on to iOS devices including the role of WebDriverAgent. We delved into what a WebDriverAgent is and how it facilitates communication from the Appium server and provide step-by-step guide on building and configuring WebDriverAgent, with special attention to Apple's code signing process.

CHAPTER 4

All About Desired Capabilities

What Will You Learn

In this chapter, you will learn the fundamentals of desired capabilities and their crucial role in initiating an Appium session. You'll understand how they serve as the bridge between your test scripts and the Appium server, enabling precise communication. The chapter will cover platform-specific capabilities for Android and iOS, guiding you through the configuration of essential fields such as platformName, deviceName, and automationName. You will also explore advanced concepts like the alwaysMatch and firstMatch strategies from the W3C WebDriver protocol, learning how to organize capabilities efficiently for diverse testing scenarios. Additionally, the chapter delves into setting up desired capabilities for cloud providers, with a focus on leveraging cloud:appiumOptions for seamless integration. By the end, you'll be equipped with practical examples, troubleshooting tips, and best practices to ensure your configurations are robust and adaptable for real-world applications.

What Are Desired Capabilities?

Desired capabilities are a set of key-value pairs used to define the environment in which an Appium test session will execute. They act as the handshake between your test scripts and the Appium server, ensuring that the correct platform, device, and app configurations are set before a test begins. Without desired capabilities, the Appium server wouldn't know how to execute your tests or which environment to target.

For example, desired capabilities specify whether the test should run on an Android or iOS device, whether the app under test is installed locally or is available via a URL, and which automation engine to use (e.g., UiAutomator2 for Android or XCUITest for iOS). By explicitly defining these parameters, you ensure consistent and predictable test execution.

Types of Capabilities

1. Standard Capabilities

These are defined by the W3C WebDriver specification and form the baseline for any Appium test. Examples include

- platformName: Specifies the platform under test (e.g., Android or iOS)
- browserName: Indicates if the test involves a mobile browser, such as Chrome or Safari

Standard capabilities are essential for ensuring compatibility with the WebDriver protocol.

2. Appium-Specific Capabilities

In addition to the standard set, Appium introduces its own capabilities to provide extended functionality. These are prefixed with appium: to differentiate them from the W3C standard. Examples include

- appium:automationName: Specifies the automation engine to use, such as UiAutomator2 for Android or XCUITest for iOS
- appium:deviceName: Defines the name or type of the device under test
- appium:app: Indicates the path to the mobile application under test

The use of the appium: prefix is crucial when defining these capabilities, as omitting it may cause compatibility issues with the WebDriver protocol.

The list of all the capabilities for Android can be found here: https://github.com/appium/appium-uiautomator2-driver?tab=readme-ov-file#capabilities.

The list of all the capabilities for iOS can be found here: https://appium.github.io/appium-xcuitest-driver/latest/reference/capabilities/.

3. Cloud-Specific Capabilities

When executing tests on cloud platforms, additional capabilities specific to the provider are often required. For example, cloud providers like LambdaTest or BrowserStack use a lt:options for LambdaTest and bs:options for BrowserStack capability to group provider-specific settings. This feature enables you to configure parameters such as session IDs, credentials, and regional preferences, while standard capabilities remain at the top level.

4. Mandatory Capabilities

Certain capabilities must always be defined to initiate a session. These include

- platformName: Specifies the platform to be tested, such as Android or iOS
- automationName: Indicates the automation engine to be used, such as UiAutomator2 for Android or XCUITest for iOS

Without these mandatory capabilities, the Appium server will not be able to establish a test session.

5. Cloud Provider Integration

When running tests on cloud providers, the configuration often extends beyond local setups. A typical cloud integration might involve separating standard capabilities from cloud-specific ones:

Standard capabilities at the top level

```
{
  "appium:platformName": "iOS",
  "appium:deviceName": "iPhone 14",
  "appium:automationName": "XCUITest"
}
```

Cloud-specific capabilities under cloud:appiumOptions, for example, if you run tests on LambdaTest, then the below example works.

```
{
  "lt:options": {
    "sessionName": "iOS Regression Test",
    "buildName": "iOS 15.0 Build",
    "user": "yourUsername",
    "accessKey": "yourAccessKey"
  }
}
```

This structure simplifies the maintenance of compatibility across multiple environments by encapsulating provider-specific details.

Capabilities for Parallel Execution

When executing tests in parallel across multiple Android and iOS devices, it's critical to set up specific capabilities to ensure the tests are executed without errors. These capabilities act as configurations to uniquely identify each session and device, preventing conflicts during the test execution. Parallel execution is an essential strategy for optimizing test runtime, especially when dealing with multiple devices or operating systems.

Appium provides two main approaches for handling parallel test execution:

1. Per-Process Approach

In this approach, multiple Appium server processes are started, each running on a unique port. Each server instance is responsible for managing a single session, tied to a specific device. For example, you can start multiple Appium servers using different command-line arguments to specify the port and device configuration.

- **Advantages**
  - Provides complete isolation between sessions
  - Suitable for scenarios where devices have distinct setups or environments

- **Disadvantages**
  - Resource-intensive, as each server instance consumes memory and processing power
  - Requires manual management of multiple server processes, which can become complex in larger test setups

2. Per-Request Approach (Preferred Method)

This approach allows a single Appium server process to manage multiple sessions simultaneously. Each session corresponds to a separate device, identified by unique capabilities such as `udid` (unique device identifier).

- **Advantages**
  - **Resource Efficiency**: Uses fewer system resources since only one server process is running
  - **Simplified Management**: Easier to configure and maintain, especially for large-scale parallel executions
  - **Better Control**: Provides improved handling of sessions, ensuring that resource allocation is optimized

3. Key Capabilities for Parallel Execution

When configuring parallel execution, the following capabilities are essential to uniquely identify each session and device:

1. `udid`: Specifies the unique identifier for the iOS/Android device. This ensures that the test session connects to the correct device.
2. `systemPort` (Android): Set a unique system port number for each parallel session. Otherwise, you might get a port conflict for UIAutomator2.
3. `wdaLocalPort` (iOS): Assigns a unique port for WebDriverAgent to ensure multiple iOS devices can be tested simultaneously.
4. `chromeDriverPort` (Android): The unique chromeDriver port if testing WebViews or Chrome and this is not applicable for iOS.

4. Best Practices for Parallel Execution

- Use the **per-request approach** for most scenarios, as it simplifies the setup and minimizes resource consumption.

- Ensure unique capability values for each device in your test suite to avoid conflicts.

- Use tools like Appium Device Farm or Selenium Grid to manage multiple Appium driver instances efficiently in larger setups. Appium device is a plugin that is build using plugin architecture of Appium, and it enables users to just plug their devices and not worry about port management or session management during parallel testing.

- Validate device connectivity and capability configurations before triggering the tests to prevent runtime errors.

By leveraging these approaches and properly configuring your test environment, you can achieve seamless parallel test execution, significantly reduce your test cycle time, and improve overall efficiency.

Summary

In this chapter, you explored the fundamentals of **desired capabilities** in Appium and their essential role in establishing a test session. Desired capabilities act as a bridge between test scripts and the Appium server, ensuring precise communication and correct configuration.

You learned about different types of capabilities:

- **Standard capabilities** (defined by W3C WebDriver, e.g., platformName, browserName)

- **Appium-specific capabilities** (prefixed with appium:, e.g., appium:automationName, appium:deviceName)

- **Cloud-specific capabilities**, where cloud providers use cloud:appiumOptions for additional configurations

- **Mandatory capabilities** like platformName and automationName, which are required for initiating a session

Additionally, the chapter covered **cloud provider integration**, showing how to structure capabilities for cloud-based execution while maintaining compatibility across environments.

Finally, you learned about **parallel execution strategies**, including

- The **per-process approach**, which runs separate Appium server instances per device.

- The **per-request approach**, which allows a single Appium server to manage multiple sessions efficiently.

Key capabilities like `udid`, `systemPort`, and `wdaLocalPort` were discussed to ensure smooth parallel execution without conflicts.

By applying these concepts, you can configure Appium sessions effectively, optimize test execution, and integrate seamlessly with cloud providers.

CHAPTER 5

How to Inspect Elements

What Will You Learn

In this chapter, you will gain a comprehensive understanding of inspecting elements for both Android and iOS applications. You will explore the various types of locators, learning their unique purposes and the best ways to utilize them in your test automation efforts. Additionally, this chapter delves into the functionalities and features of Appium Inspector, highlighting how they can streamline your workflow. Finally, this chapter guides you through practical steps for using Appium Inspector effectively, along with valuable tips to maximize its potential in your automation projects.

How to Install Inspector

There are two ways to install appium-inspector: one way is as installer and the other as plugin, which will be available from Appium 3.0.

Let's first see how to install appium-inspector as an installer. Download the package that is suitable for your machine (https://github.com/appium/appium-inspector/releases/).

In our case, we will download dmg for mac and install the package. Open the installed package. You should see session builder screen as in Figure 5-1.

CHAPTER 5   HOW TO INSPECT ELEMENTS

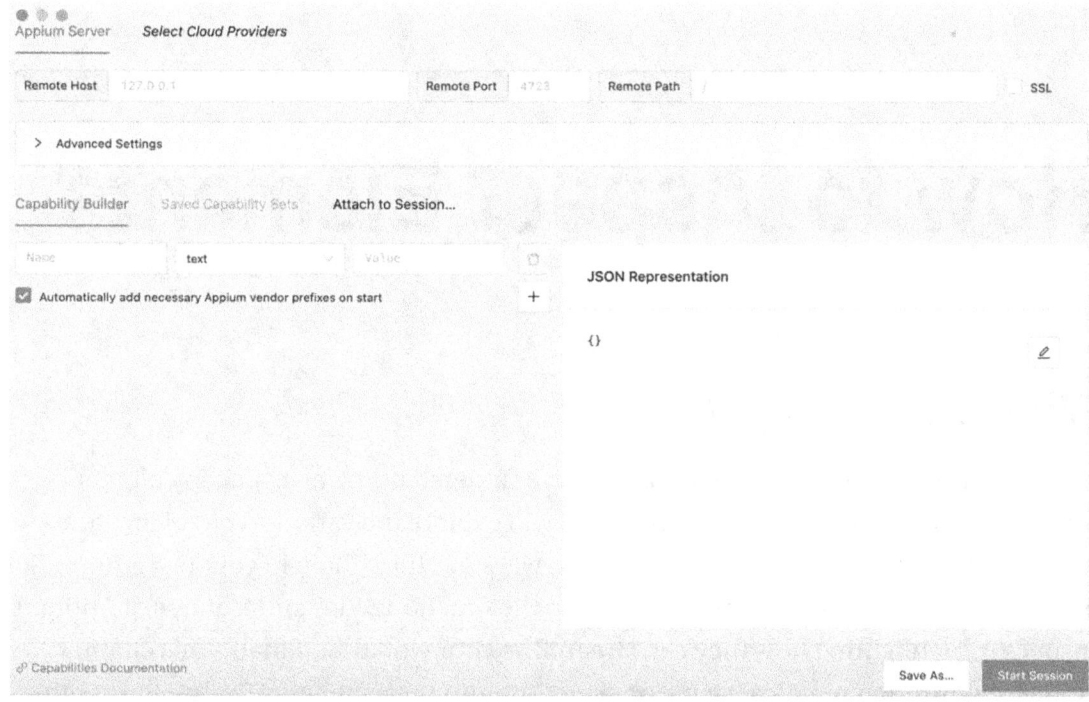

Figure 5-1. Session builder

The session builder screen consists of four key sections:

1. **Server Details**: This section requires the Appium server URL and the corresponding port number, along with the base path. By default, the server communicates over HTTP, but you can enable HTTPS by selecting the provided checkbox.

2. **Capability Builder**: Here, you can add all the platform-specific capabilities required to create a new automation session.

3. **Saved Capabilities**: This section allows you to save the capabilities configured in the capability builder for future reuse, streamlining session creation.

4. **Attach to Session**: Use this tab if an automation session is already running, enabling you to inspect elements within the existing session.

5. **Select Cloud Providers**: Selecting the cloud provider tab enables you to create a session on respective cloud vendors like LambdaTest, Sauce Labs, HeadSpin, and more.

Create a Session for Android and iOS

We will walk through the process of creating a session for both Android and iOS applications. This guide will cover setting up sessions for local execution, where tests are run on devices or emulators connected to your local machine. Additionally, we will explore how to configure sessions for cloud execution, which allows you to run tests on cloud-based platforms such as LambdaTest, Sauce Labs, or other similar services. By the end of this section, you will have a clear understanding of how to create and manage sessions tailored to your specific execution environment.

First, you need to start an Appium server in your terminal. Open terminal and run the command

```
appium server --base-path=/wd/hub
```

Once the Appium server is up and running, you can begin adding all the necessary details into the session builder:

1. **Server Details**: Enter the Appium server URL and the port number on which the server was started. If you are using the default configuration, the server will be accessible at `127.0.0.1` with port `4723` and the base path set to `/wd/hub`.

2. **Capability Builder**: Configure the mandatory capabilities required for both iOS and Android platforms. These capabilities are essential to define the session's behavior and ensure successful communication between your Appium setup and the target devices.

This setup process ensures that your session is configured correctly, enabling you to proceed with automation tasks seamlessly.

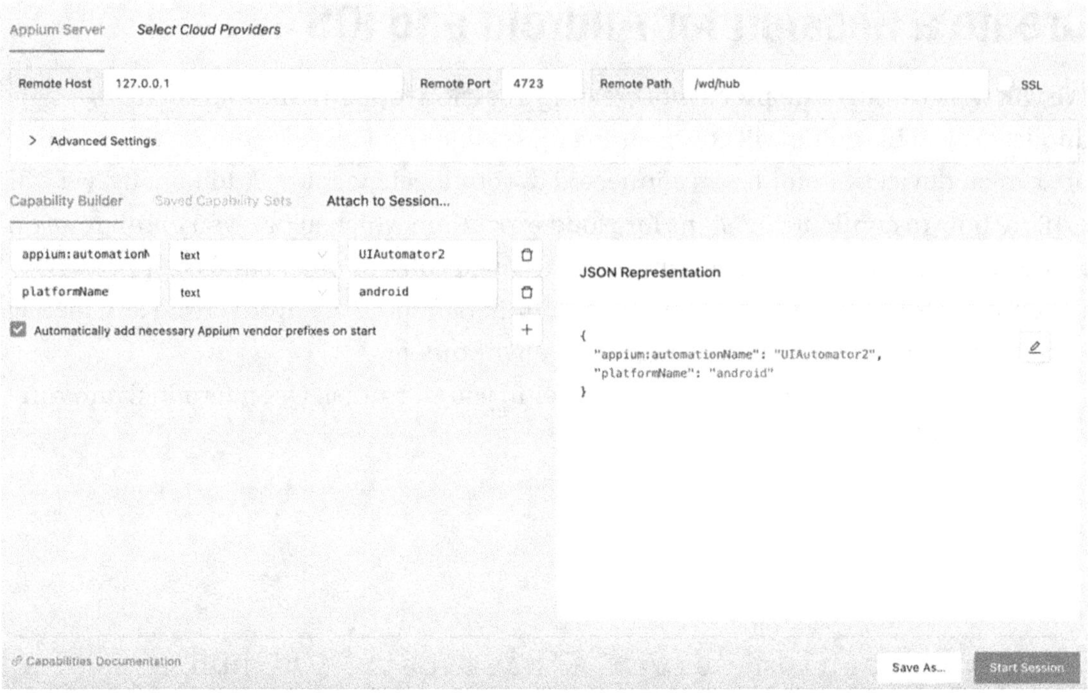

CHAPTER 5   HOW TO INSPECT ELEMENTS

Figure 5-2. Android capabilities

Now, before clicking on Start Session, make sure the Android emulator or a real device is connected to the machine.

Start Session will establish a connection to the Appium server with the capabilities specified. Refer to Figure 5-3.

CHAPTER 5   HOW TO INSPECT ELEMENTS

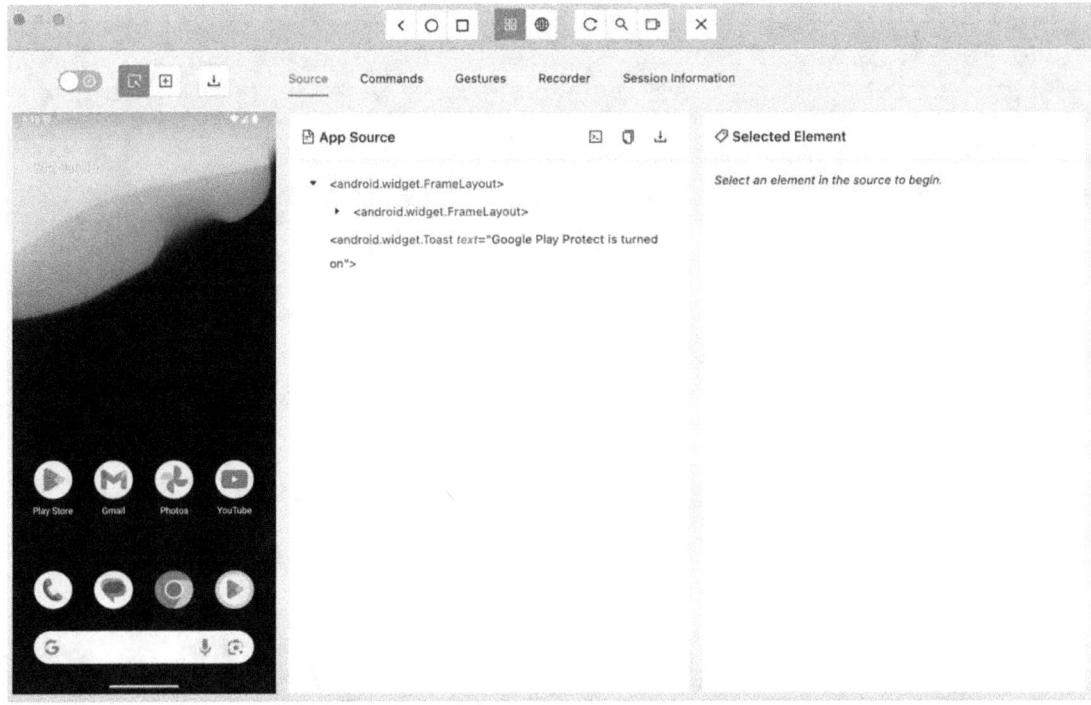

Figure 5-3. *Android session creation*

If you want Appium to start an Android emulator automatically, you can use the appium:avdName capability which was created by Android Studio under Android Specific Requirement section. This capability allows you to specify the name of the Android Virtual Device (AVD) that Appium should start. By providing the avdName, you ensure that Appium launches the exact emulator you need for your tests.

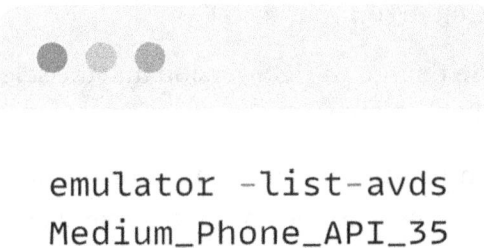

```
emulator -list-avds
Medium_Phone_API_35
```

Let's go ahead and see how to create a session for iOS simulators; for this, we just need to change the capabilities that fit iOS. Refer to Figure 5-4.

75

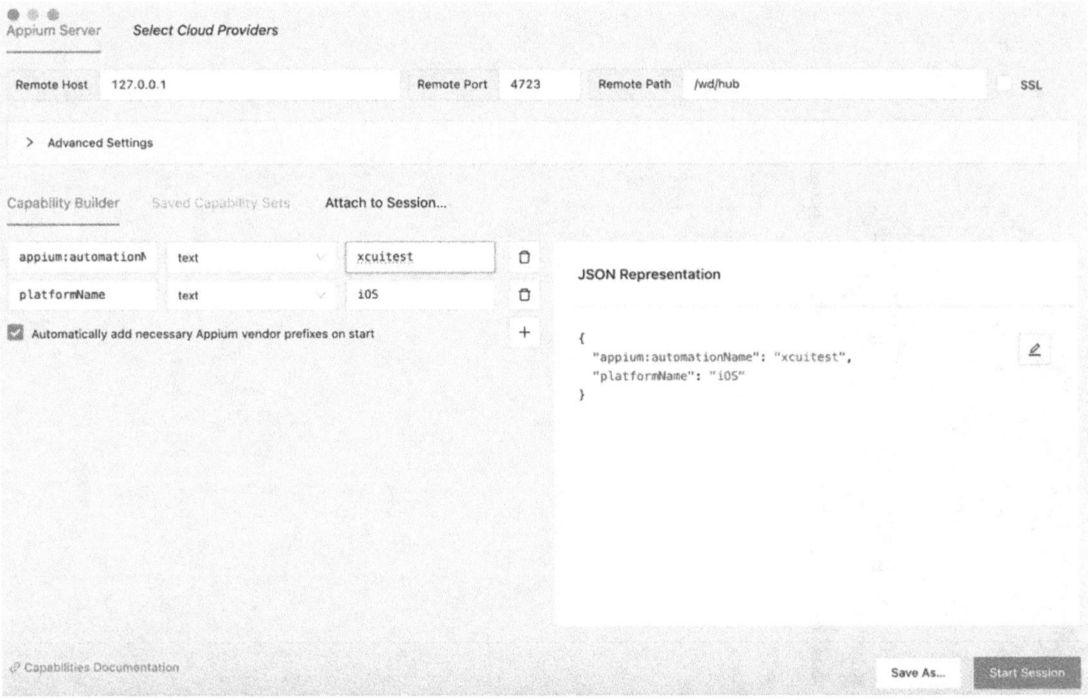

Chapter 5 How to Inspect Elements

Figure 5-4. iOS capabilities

When you click the **Start Session** button, Appium begins by evaluating the desired capabilities that have been provided. Desired capabilities are key-value pairs that tell Appium what type of session to initiate. Among these, two critical capabilities for iOS testing are **deviceName** and **platformVersion**.

- **deviceName** specifies the name of the iOS simulator or real device on which you want to run your tests.

- **platformVersion** defines the iOS version that the selected device or simulator should be running.

If both **deviceName** and **platformVersion** are provided in the desired capabilities, Appium uses them to locate and start the appropriate simulator or device. However, if these details are omitted, Appium will fall back to its default behavior. In such cases, it will automatically select the first available iOS simulator from the list of configured simulators and use it to start the session. Refer to Figure 5-5.

CHAPTER 5   HOW TO INSPECT ELEMENTS

```
[XCUITestDriver@e6a6] 'platformVersion' capability ('undefined') is not a valid version number.
 Consider fixing it or be ready to experience an inconsistent driver behavior.
[8b6f0543][XCUITestDriver@e6a6] Session created with session id: 8b6f0543-9d1e-4184-8750-8dda3fcd1fd8
[8b6f0543][XCUITest] Current user: 'saikrishna'
[8b6f0543][XCUITestDriver@e6a6] No real device udid has been provided in capabilities.
 Will select a matching simulator to run the test.
[8b6f0543][XCUITestDriver@e6a6] iOS SDK Version set to '18.2'
[8b6f0543][XCUITestDriver@e6a6] No platformVersion specified. Using the latest version Xcode supports: '18.2'.
 This may cause problems if a simulator does not exist for this platform version.
 Looking for an existing Simulator with platformName: iOS, platformVersion: 18.2, deviceName: undefined
 The 'deviceName' capability value is empty. Selecting the first matching device 'iPhone 16 Pro' having the 'platformVersion' set to 18.2
[8b6f0543][XCUITestDriver@e6a6] Constructing iOS simulator for Xcode version 16.2 with udid 'E9F10A3E-58E6-4506-B273-B22AF836014E'
```

Figure 5-5. *iOS server logs*

Once the Appium server finds the respective iOS simulator version, it takes care of booting and installing WDA (WebDriverAgent) and the session is successfully created. Refer to Figure 5-6.

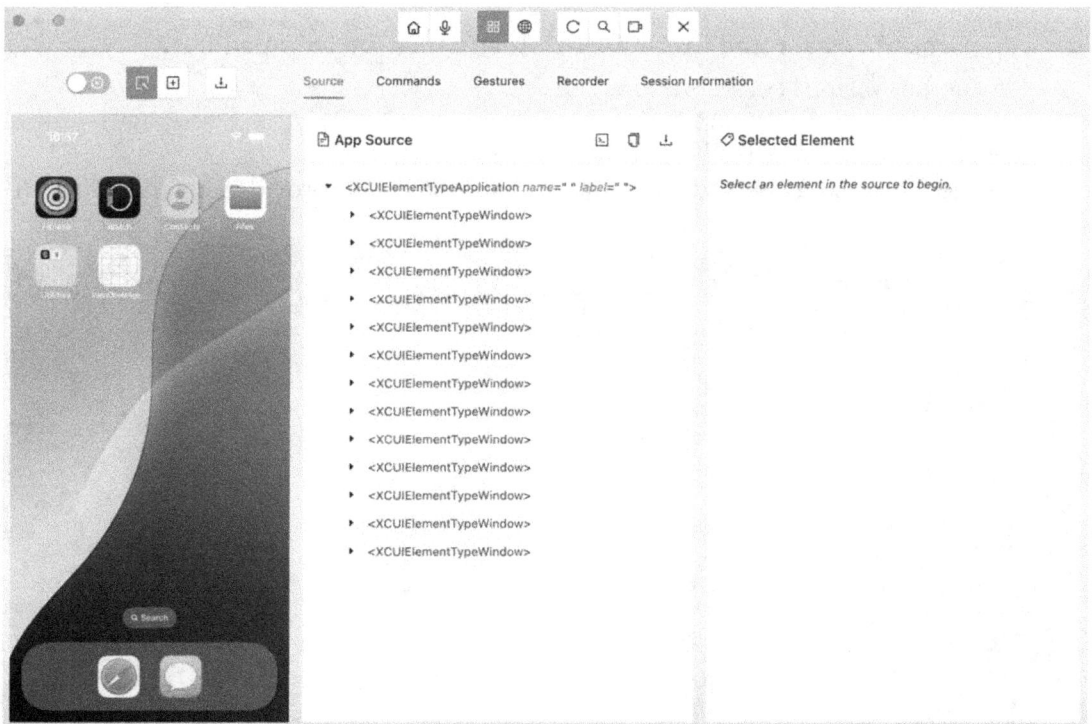

Figure 5-6. *iOS session creation*

As we've explored using the Appium Inspector to create a session on a local device, let's now move on to leveraging cloud-based devices to achieve the same. Cloud-based testing platforms provide access to a wide range of devices and operating systems, enabling you to run tests on configurations that may not be available locally.

There are several cloud vendors available, such as Sauce Labs, BrowserStack, and LambdaTest, among others. In this section, we'll choose one of these vendors and walk through the process of setting up a session on a cloud device.

Why Use Cloud Devices?

Cloud devices offer several advantages:

1. **Scalability**: Test on multiple devices simultaneously

2. **Wide Device Availability**: Access a broad range of devices and OS versions

3. **Convenience**: No need to maintain physical devices or emulators locally

4. **Cross-Browser and Cross-Device Testing**: Ensure compatibility across various configurations

Let's pick LambdaTest as the cloud provider.

Click the Select Cloud Providers and select LambdaTest as provider. Refer to Figure 5-7.

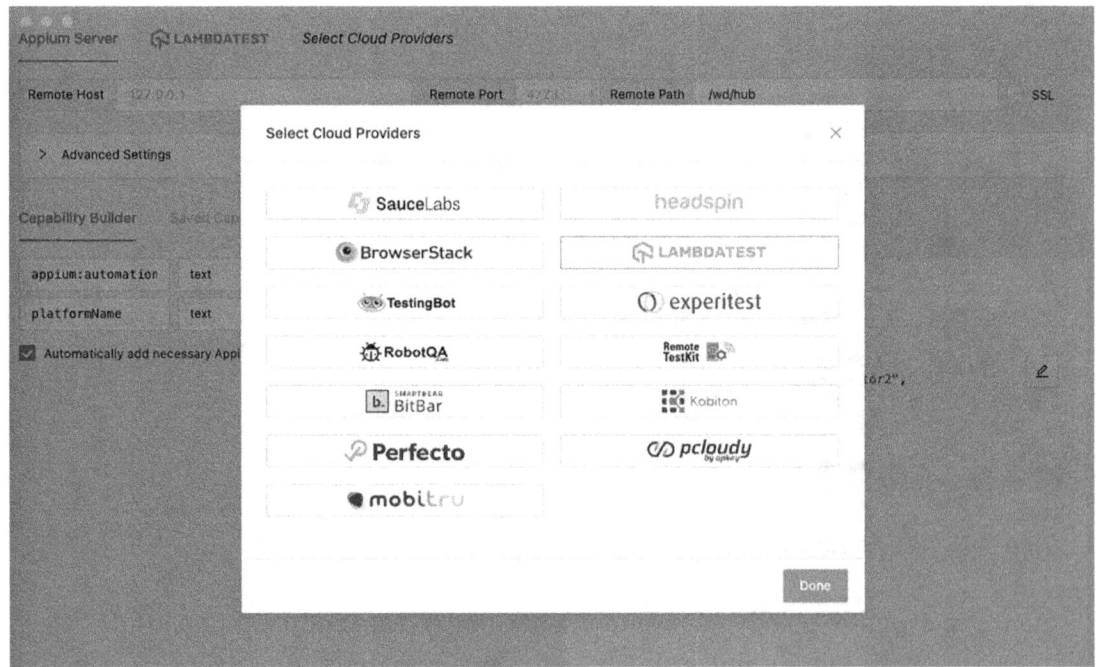

Figure 5-7. Cloud providers

Step 1: Create a LambdaTest Account

To use Appium Inspector with LambdaTest, you first need an account. Navigate to LambdaTest's website and sign up for a free or paid account.

Step 2: Retrieve Your LambdaTest Credentials

Once your account is created, you'll need your **Username** and **Access Key** to authenticate your session with LambdaTest. Follow these steps to retrieve them:

1. Log in to your LambdaTest Dashboard.

2. Click your **Profile Icon** in the bottom-left corner.

3. Copy your **Username** and **Access Key**.

Refer to Figure 5-8 for a visual reference on where to find these credentials.

CHAPTER 5   HOW TO INSPECT ELEMENTS

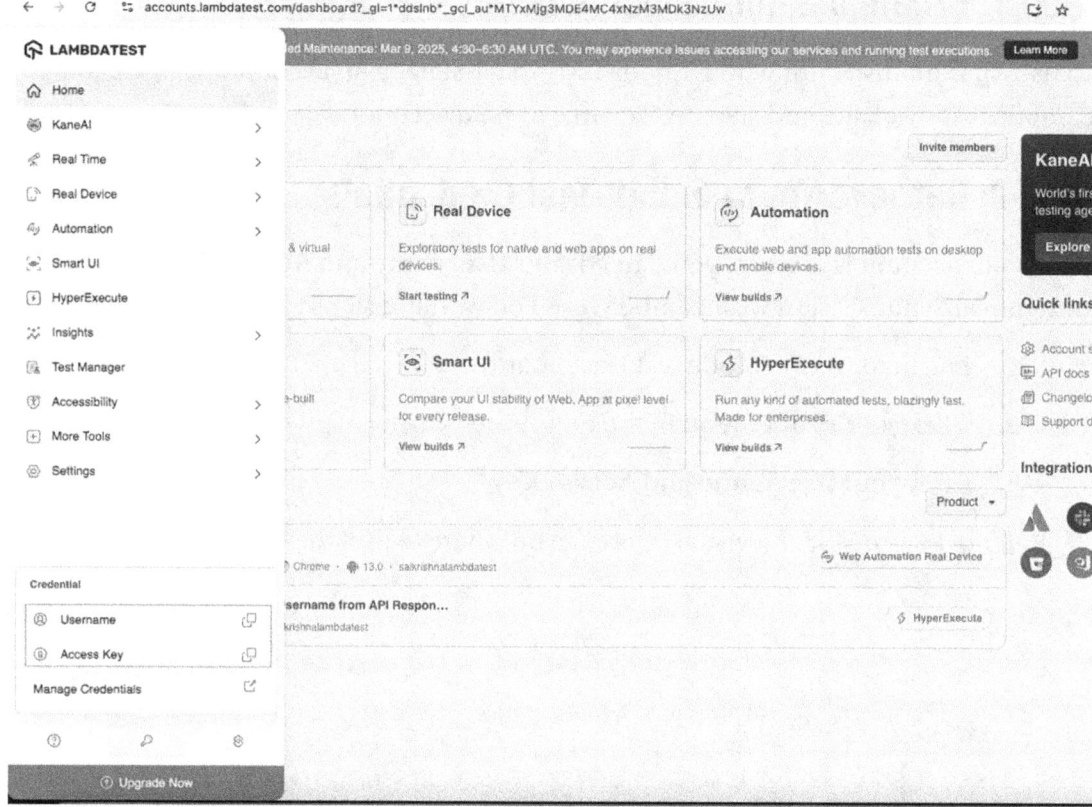

Figure 5-8.   LT creds

Step 3: Define the Required Capabilities

To create a successful Appium session with LambdaTest, you need to define the correct **desired capabilities**. These capabilities help specify key details such as the target platform, device, application, and automation framework. They ensure that LambdaTest provisions the right cloud device for your test session.

Using LambdaTest's Capability Generator

LambdaTest provides a **Capability Generator** tool that simplifies the process of defining desired capabilities. Instead of manually writing the JSON, you can generate it dynamically based on your test requirements.

Visit the **LambdaTest Capability Generator** (https://www.lambdatest.com/capabilities-generator/) and follow these steps:

1. Select the **Platform** (Android or iOS).

2. Choose a **Device** from the available list.

3. Select the **Operating System version**.

4. Specify the **Appium version** (if needed).

5. Provide the **App ID** (obtained after uploading your app).

6. Generate the JSON and copy the output.

Uploading the App to LambdaTest

Before starting the session, you need to upload your application to LambdaTest's cloud storage. This will generate a unique **App ID**, which you must include in your desired capabilities.

To upload an app:

1. Log in to your **LambdaTest Dashboard**.

2. Navigate to the **App Testing** section.

3. Click **Upload** and select your `.apk` or `.ipa` file.

4. Once uploaded, LambdaTest will generate an **App ID** (e.g., `lt://APP123huij4343`).

5. Copy this App ID and include it in the desired capabilities under the `"app"` key.

Enter all these values in the Appium Inspector. Refer to Figure 5-9.

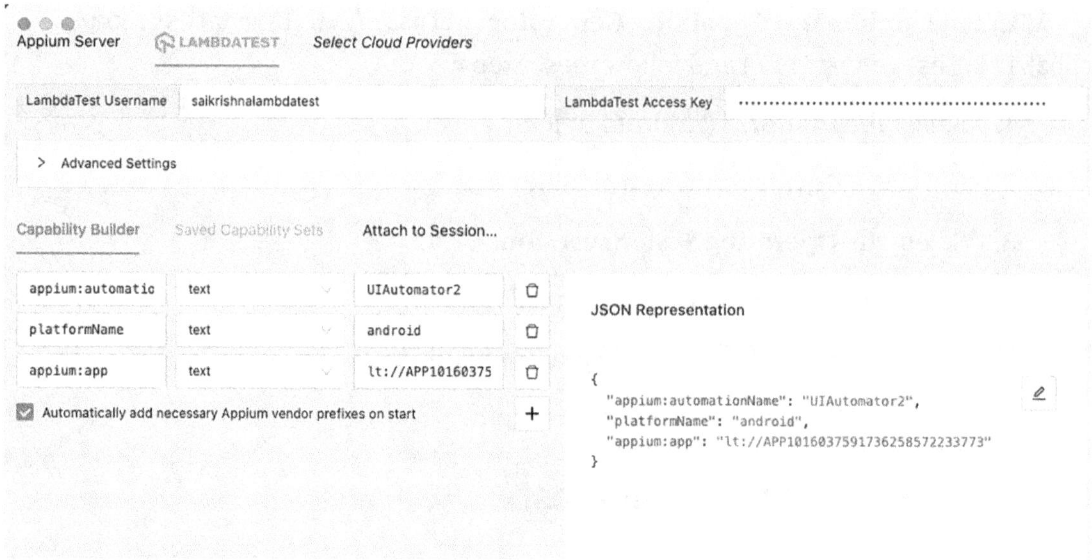

CHAPTER 5   HOW TO INSPECT ELEMENTS

Figure 5-9. LT capabilities

How the Session Works

Once these capabilities are set up and a session is initiated:

- LambdaTest will **automatically allocate an available device** matching your configuration.

- An **Appium session** will be created in LambdaTest's cloud.

- You can now interact with the app, inspect UI elements, and execute automated tests remotely.

This ensures a seamless testing experience, allowing you to debug and inspect your mobile app on different cloud devices without needing a physical device locally.

Now that we have successfully created Appium sessions for both **Android and iOS** on **local devices** and **cloud providers (such as LambdaTest)**, the next step is to explore **element inspection**. This is a crucial part of mobile automation testing, as it allows us to locate UI elements and understand their properties before writing automation scripts.

Exploring Appium Inspector

Appium Inspector provides a visual interface to inspect elements on the mobile app, view their attributes, and generate locator strategies for use in test scripts.

CHAPTER 5 HOW TO INSPECT ELEMENTS

Once your session is active, Appium Inspector provides multiple functionalities to help with UI inspection.

View the Mobile App Hierarchy

- The **App Source** panel displays the complete **UI hierarchy** of the mobile application in XML format.
- This hierarchical structure is similar to HTML DOM in web testing, showing how elements are nested.

Selecting Elements for Android

- Click any **UI element** within the mirrored device screen to highlight it in the App Source. Refer to Figure 5-10.

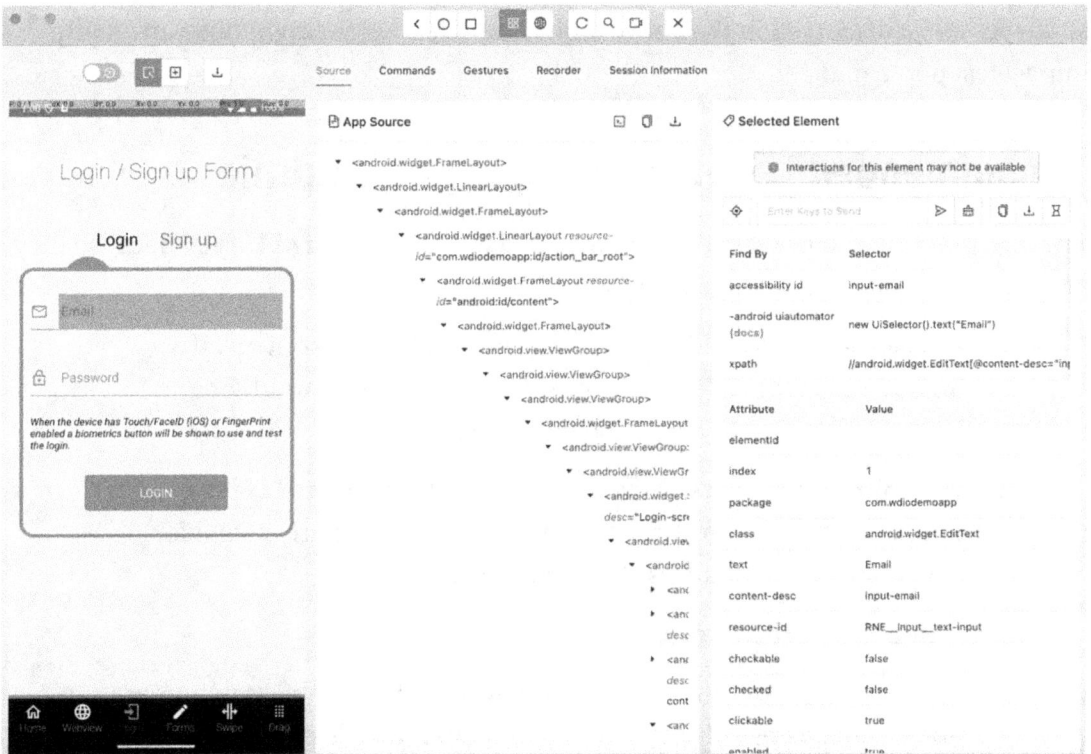

Figure 5-10. *Android-inspected element*

- The **selected element's attributes** (such as ID, class, text, bounds, and accessibility properties) will be displayed in the **Attributes Panel**.

Locator strategy	Usage
id	`RNE__Input__text-input`: Use if it's unique and stable.
className	`android.widget.EditText`: Locates elements by class type but may return multiple results.
xpath	`//android.widget.EditText[@content-desc='input-email']`: Use only when other locators are not available; slower performance.
accessibilityId	`"input-email"`: Recommended as it's faster and reliable.

When writing automation scripts, it's crucial to choose the most efficient locator strategy to interact with UI elements. A well-optimized locator strategy improves script stability, execution speed, and overall test reliability. Appium supports multiple locator strategies as we discussed in the above table, and selecting the right one can greatly impact test performance.

Recommended Locator Strategies for Android

The best practice is to prioritize **ID (`resource-id`) and `accessibilityId`** because they are the fastest and most reliable locators.

1. **ID (`resource-id`)**: This is the most efficient locator strategy. If a unique `resource-id` is available for an element (Android) or a name (iOS), it should always be the first choice.

2. **accessibilityId (`content-desc` or `accessibilityIdentifier`)**: This is another fast and stable method. It is particularly useful for elements meant for accessibility support.

Avoid Using Unreliable Strategies

- **className (`android.widget.EditText`, etc.)**: Since class names are not unique, using this method may lead to multiple elements being returned, which makes finding the right element more difficult.

CHAPTER 5 HOW TO INSPECT ELEMENTS

- **XPath** (`//android.widget.EditText[@content-desc="input-email"]`): XPath should only be used when no other reliable locators are available. XPath queries are slower and can cause flakiness due to dynamic element hierarchies.

Selecting Elements for iOS

- Click any **UI element** within the mirrored device screen to highlight it in the App Source. Refer to Figure 5-11.

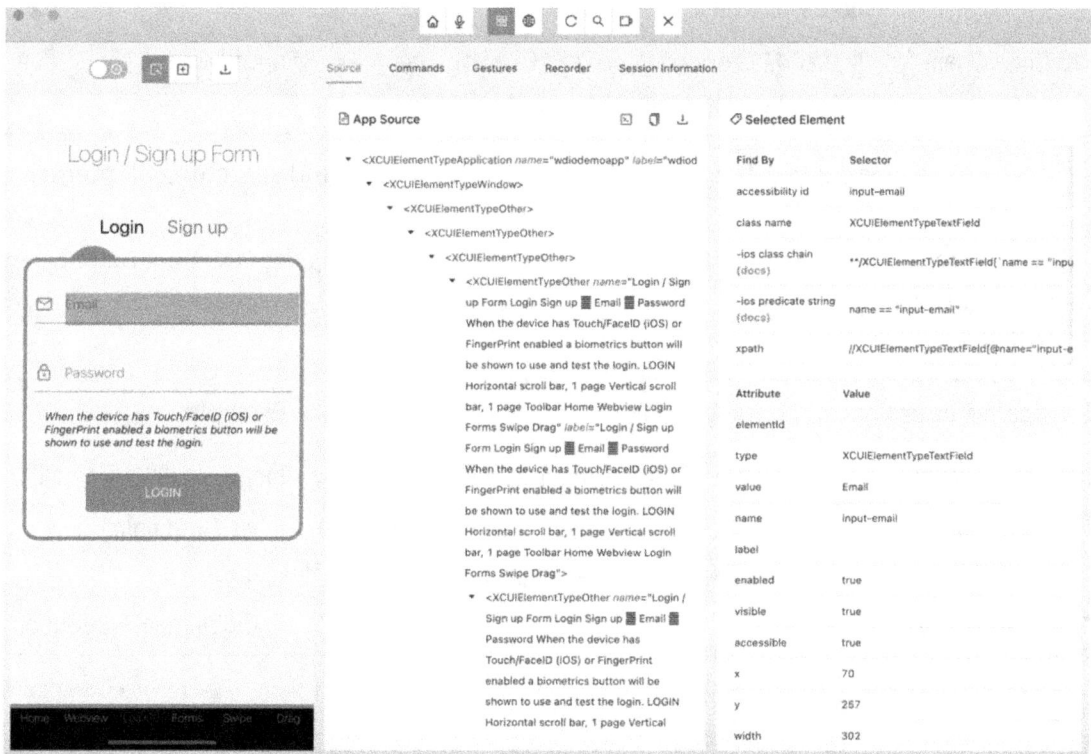

Figure 5-11. iOS-inspect element

- The **selected element's attributes** (such as ID, class, text, bounds, and accessibility properties) will be displayed in the **Attributes Panel**.

85

CHAPTER 5   HOW TO INSPECT ELEMENTS

Locator strategy	Usage
id	`input-email`: Use if it's unique and stable.
className	`XCUIElementTypeTextField`: Locates elements by class type but may return multiple results.
xpath	`//XCUIElementTypeTextField[@name='input-email']`: Use only when other locators are not available; slower performance.
accessibilityId	`"input-email"`: Recommended as it's faster and reliable.
NS Predicate String	`name == "input-email"`: Efficient for locating elements when accessibilityId is not available.
iOS Class Chain	`**/XCUIElementTypeTextField[\name == "input-email"`]`: Can be used for hierarchical element selection.

NSPredicate is a query language used in iOS for filtering and searching elements efficiently.

It is widely used in **Appium** for iOS automation when using the **iOS Predicate String** locator strategy.

Basic Syntax

Predicate expression	Description	Example
name == "value"	Matches an element with the exact name	name == "input-email"
label == "value"	Matches an element with the exact label	label == "Login"
type == "XCUIElementTypeTextField"	Finds elements by type/class	type == "XCUIElementTypeButton"

String Matching

Predicate expression	Description	Example
name CONTAINS "text"	Contains substring (case-sensitive)	name CONTAINS "email"
name CONTAINS[c] "text"	Contains substring (case-insensitive)	name CONTAINS[c] "EMAIL"
name BEGINSWITH "text"	Starts with a specific text	name BEGINSWITH "input"
name ENDSWITH "text"	Ends with a specific text	name ENDSWITH "email"
name MATCHES "regex"	Matches a regex pattern	name MATCHES ".*email.*"

Logical Operators

Predicate expression	Description
name == "Login" AND enabled == true	Finds enabled elements with a specific name
name == "Submit" OR name == "Save"	Finds elements with either nam
NOT name == "Cancel"	Excludes an element with a specific name

Finding Multiple Elements

Predicate expression	Description
type == "XCUIElementTypeButton" AND visible == true	Finds all visible button
(name == "Login" OR name == "Sign up") AND enabled == true	Finds elements that match either name and are enabled

Next, let's explore another important iOS locator strategy called **iOS Class Chain**. It is a query format used in WebDriverAgent that functions similarly to XPath but is more optimized for iOS automation. It leverages **XCUIElementQuery** methods, allowing indexing and predicate-based filtering for more flexible and efficient element searches.

Here are some examples that mirror **iOS Class Chain** queries with **WebDriverAgent's** lookup syntax:

Basic Examples

Class chain expression	Description
XCUIElementTypeWindow/ XCUIElementTypeButton[3]	Selects the **third button** that is a **direct child** of the **first window**
XCUIElementTypeWindow	Selects **all child windows** at the first level
XCUIElementTypeWindow[2]	Selects the **second child window** (indexing starts at 1)
XCUIElementTypeWindow/ XCUIElementTypeAny[3]	Selects the **third child (any type)** of the **first window**
XCUIElementTypeWindow[2]/ XCUIElementTypeAny[-2]	Selects the **second-last child** of the **second window**

Using Predicates in Queries

Class chain expression	Description
XCUIElementTypeWindow[name CONTAINS[cd] "blabla"]	Selects all **windows** where the name contains "blabla" (case-insensitive)
XCUIElementTypeWindow[label BEGINSWITH "blabla"][-1]	Selects the **last window** where the label begins with "blabla"
XCUIElementTypeWindow/ XCUIElementTypeAny[value == "bla1" OR label == "bla2"]	Selects **all children** of the **first window** where `value == "bla1" OR label == "bla2"`
XCUIElementTypeWindow[name == "you're the winner"]/XCUIElementTypeAny[visible == 1]	Selects **all visible children** of the **first window** named `"you're the winner"`

Recommended Locator Strategies for iOS

Preferred Strategies

1. **ID (name attribute in iOS):** The most efficient and reliable locator strategy

2. **accessibilityId (accessibilityIdentifier):** Designed for automation and accessibility, ensuring stable identification

3. **iOS Class Chain:** A structured way to locate elements using class hierarchy, faster than XPath

4. **NSPredicate String:** Uses Apple's predicate format to filter elements based on attributes, providing flexibility

Avoid Using Unreliable Strategies

1. **className (XCUIElementType elements):** May return multiple elements, making it less reliable

2. **XPath:** Slow, unstable, and prone to breaking with UI changes, should be a last resort

CHAPTER 5 HOW TO INSPECT ELEMENTS

Element Interaction with Inspector

Now that we have explored all the possible locator strategies available for both iOS and Android, along with practical examples of their usage, it is essential to ensure that the locators we choose are accurate and reliable before integrating them into our test automation scripts. The best way to validate the correctness of a locator is by using an element inspector, such as Appium Inspector, which allows us to interact with the application's UI hierarchy in real time. By inspecting elements, we can verify their attributes, test different locator strategies, and refine our selection to ensure stability and efficiency in our automation tests.

Create an Appium session with inspector as we discussed in Android session creation. Refer to Figure 5-3.

Click the element search icon in the inspector. Refer to Figure 5-12 which will open a search for element model.

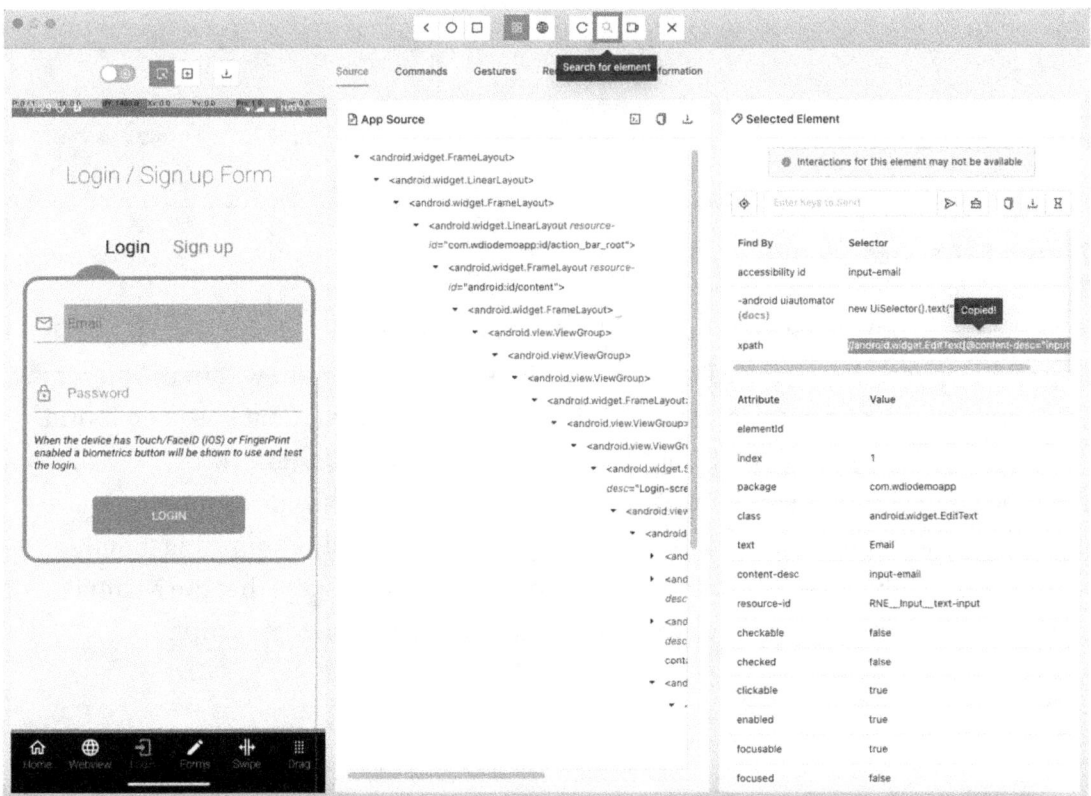

Figure 5-12. Search for element

89

Select the locator strategy and paste the selector in the input field. For example, for Android, let's select XPath and search for the xpath. Refer to Figure 5-13.

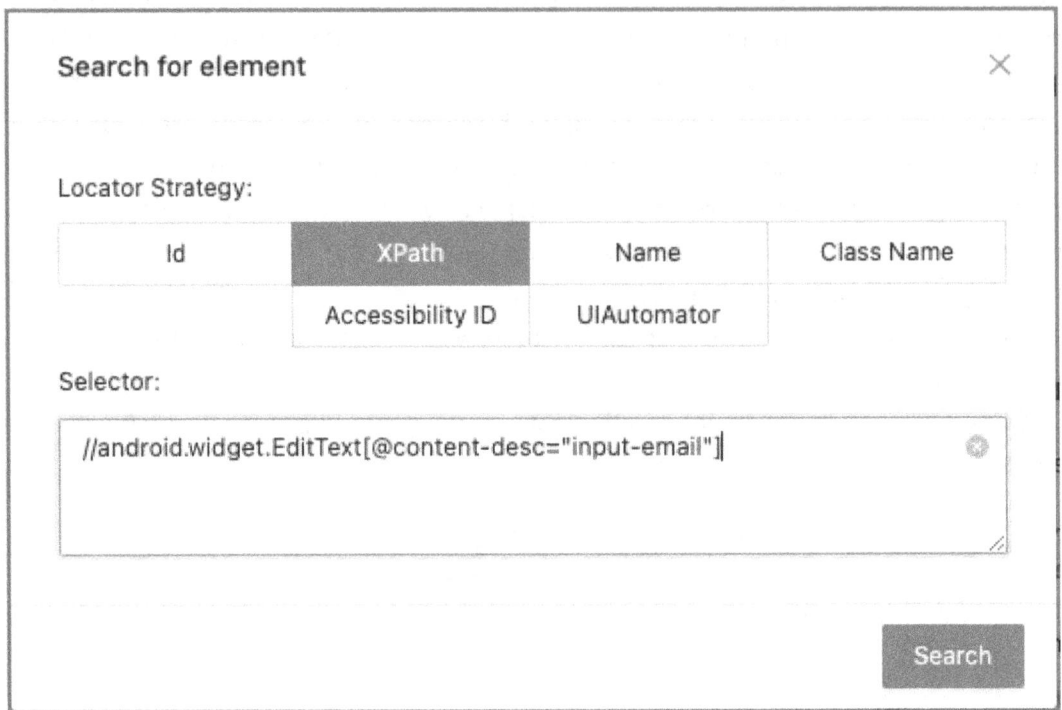

Figure 5-13. Search modal

Once you click the **Search** button, the provided XPath is validated against the DOM tree of the application. If the XPath correctly identifies an element within the hierarchy, the inspector will display a confirmation indicating that the element has been found. Additionally, the element will be associated with a **unique Element ID**.

When you click the **Element ID (Refer to Figure 5-14)**, the corresponding UI element in the application preview will be highlighted, visually confirming that the locator accurately targets the intended element. This step ensures that the XPath is precise and reliable before incorporating it into the test automation script.

CHAPTER 5   HOW TO INSPECT ELEMENTS

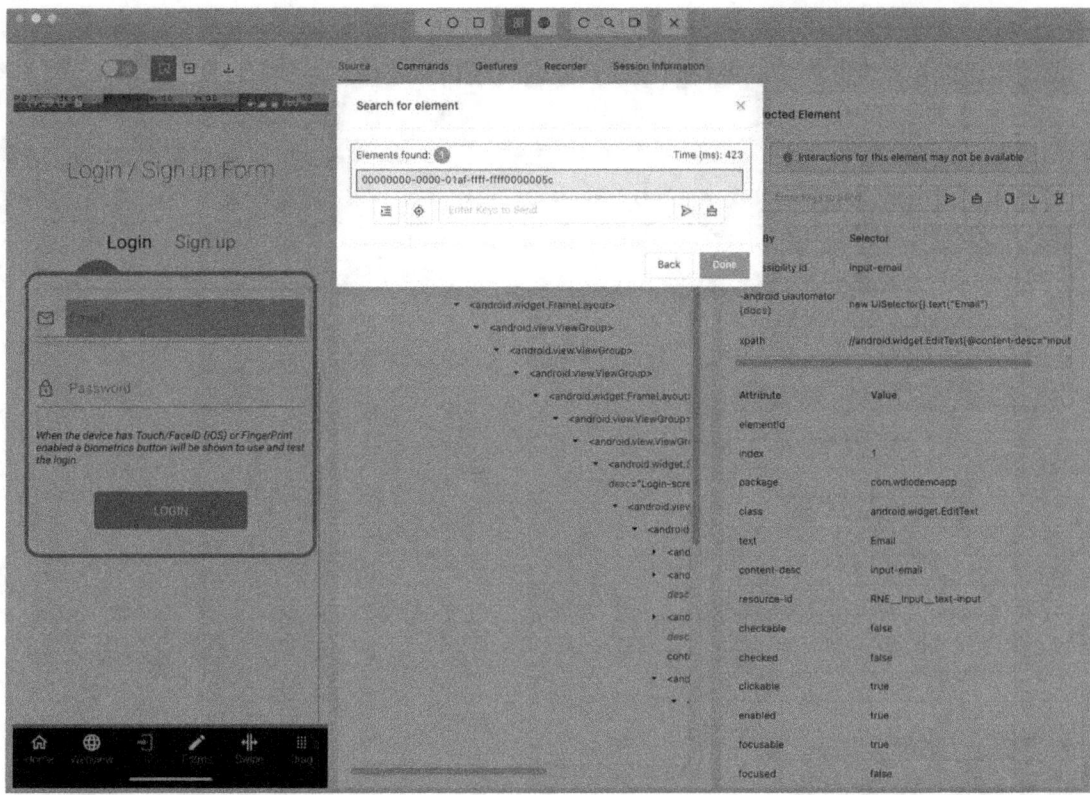

Figure 5-14. *iOS Element Locator*

Now as the element is found, you can also interact with the element like tap, sending some values into the file if it's an input field.

As we inspected the Email field which is an EditText field, we can enter value through the inspector. Refer to Figure 5-15. This way you can interact with any element and make the locator strategy works fine.

CHAPTER 5   HOW TO INSPECT ELEMENTS

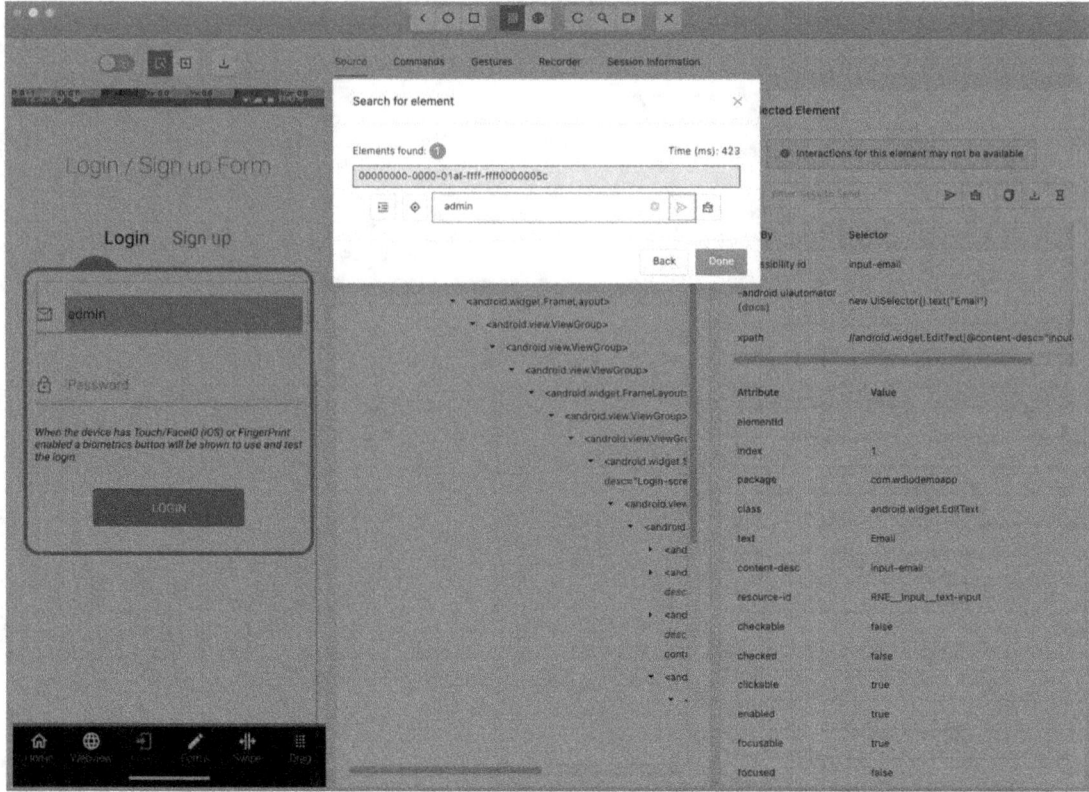

Figure 5-15. Element search

Summary

In this chapter, we explored how to effectively inspect mobile application elements using **Appium Inspector** and its integration with **LambdaTest**. We began by understanding the significance of **locators** in mobile test automation and discussed various locator strategies for **Android and iOS**, including **ID, accessibilityId, XPath, className, iOS Class Chain, and NSPredicate**.

We covered best practices for selecting the most **efficient and reliable locators**, emphasizing that **ID and accessibilityId** should be prioritized due to their speed and stability. Additionally, we highlighted why **XPath should only be used as a last resort**, as it can negatively impact test performance.

Next, we demonstrated how to use **LambdaTest's cloud-based Appium environment** to inspect mobile elements. We walked through the process of defining desired capabilities, uploading an app to LambdaTest, and establishing a remote Appium session.

Finally, we examined how to validate locator strategies within **Appium Inspector**, ensuring that selected locators uniquely identify elements before incorporating them into automation scripts. By leveraging Appium Inspector effectively, testers can build **robust and maintainable** automation frameworks, reducing flakiness and improving script reliability.

CHAPTER 6

Writing First Test

What Will You Learn

In this chapter, you will learn how to write your first Appium test using WebdriverIO (WDIO). You will start by understanding the structure of a basic test and setting up the required dependencies and configurations for both frameworks. The chapter will guide you through writing and executing a simple test case on both Android and iOS devices. You will also explore how to use WebDriver commands to interact with mobile elements and handle capabilities for session creation. Additionally, you will learn how to write assertions to validate test results and debug common issues that may arise when running your first test. By the end of this chapter, you will have a solid foundation to start automating mobile applications using Appium with WDIO.

Setting Up the Environment

Since we have already set up the necessary configurations for Appium, including **Java, Node.js, and environment variables (JAVA_HOME, ANDROID_HOME, etc.)**, we will now focus on setting up the required dependencies for writing and executing tests using **WebdriverIO (WDIO) and Java client**.

WDIO Project Setup

To write and execute Appium tests using WebdriverIO (WDIO), we need to set up a WebdriverIO project. This section will guide you through installing WDIO, configuring it, and writing your first test.

CHAPTER 6 WRITING FIRST TEST

Initialize a New WDIO Project

Open a terminal and create a new project directory, you can run the below command. Refer to Figure 6-1.

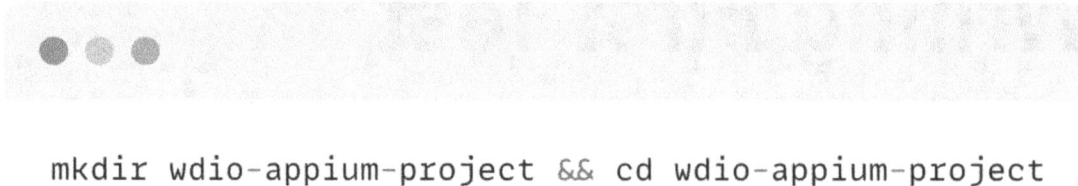

```
mkdir wdio-appium-project && cd wdio-appium-project
```

Figure 6-1. *Create project directory*

Initialize a Node.js project. Refer to Figure 6-2.

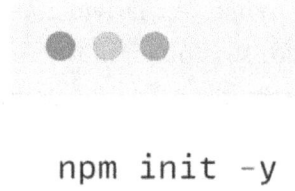

```
npm init -y
```

Figure 6-2. *Create node project*

This creates a package.json which will manage all the required dependencies for the WDIO project.

Install WebdriverIO and Required Packages

Run the following command to install WebdriverIO and Appium service dependencies. Refer to Figure 6-3.

```
npm install --save-dev webdriverio @wdio/cli @wdio/appium-service @wdio/mocha-framework chai
```

Figure 6-3. *Dependency installation*

Let's see what those dependencies do.

1. **webdriverio:** The core WebdriverIO library that enables interaction with WebDriver and Appium servers

2. **@wdio/cli:** The command-line interface for setting up, configuring, and running WebdriverIO test projects

3. **@wdio/appium-service:** A service that simplifies starting and managing the Appium server during test execution

4. **@wdio/mocha-framework:** Integrates the Mocha test framework with WebdriverIO, providing structured test execution and reporting

5. **chai:** An assertion library used for writing expressive and readable validation statements in test cases

Run the WDIO Configuration Wizard

WebdriverIO provides a setup wizard that generates a configuration file; make sure you select the options as shown in Figure 6-4.

```
npx wdio config

==================================
⭐ WDIO Configuration Wizard ⭐
==================================

✓ A project named "wdio-appium-project" was detected at "/Users/saikrishna/Documents/Book/ch-6/wdio-appium-project", correct? yes
✓ What type of testing would you like to do? E2E Testing - of Web or Mobile Applications
✓ Where is your automation backend located? On my local machine
✓ Which environment you would like to automate? Mobile - native, hybrid and mobile web apps, on Android or iOS
✓ Which mobile environment you'd like to automate? Android - native, hybrid and mobile web apps, tested on emulators and real devices
     > using UiAutomator2 (https://www.npmjs.com/package/appium-uiautomator2-driver)
✓ Which framework do you want to use? Mocha (https://mochajs.org/)
✓ Do you want to use Typescript to write tests? yes
✓ Do you want WebdriverIO to autogenerate some test files? no
✓ Which reporter do you want to use? spec
✓ Do you want to add a plugin to your test setup?
✓ Would you like to include Visual Testing to your setup? For more information see https://webdriver.io/docs/visual-testing) no
✓ Do you want to add a service to your test setup? appium
✓ Do you want me to run `npm install` yes

Setting up TypeScript...
✓ Success!
```

***Figure 6-4.** WDIO wizard setup*

CHAPTER 6   WRITING FIRST TEST

Now that we have set up the **WebdriverIO (WDIO) project**, our project directory should include the following key files and folders:

```
wdio-appium-project/
|-- node_modules/            # Contains installed dependencies
|-- test/                    # Test folder where we write test scripts
|     ├── specs/             # Contains test specifications
|     |    ├── firstTest.js  # Sample test file
|-- wdio.conf.js             # WebdriverIO configuration file
|-- package.json             # Project metadata and dependencies
|-- package-lock.json        # Dependency lock file
|-- tsconfig.json            # TypeScript configuration (if using TypeScript)
```

1. node_modules/—Dependencies Folder

This folder contains all the **npm packages** installed as dependencies for WebdriverIO, Appium, and other libraries.

- You don't need to manually modify anything inside node_modules.

- If you accidentally delete this folder, you can restore it by running npm install.

2. test/—Test Folder

This folder stores all test scripts.

- **specs**/: Contains individual test files

```
import { expect } from 'chai';
describe('First Appium Test', () => {
    it('should launch the app and verify an element', async () => {
        //Using xpath as the app didn't any any recommended locators.
        const loginButton = await $('//android.widget.TextView[@
        text="Login"]');
        expect(await loginButton.isDisplayed()).to.be.true;
    });
});
```

98

3. `wdio.conf.js`—WebdriverIO Configuration File

The wdio.conf.js file defines how WebdriverIO runs tests, specifying test files, capabilities, timeouts, and services.

4. `package.json`—Project Metadata and Dependencies

The package.json file contains project details and the installed **npm dependencies**.

```
{
  "name": "wdio-appium-project",
  "version": "1.0.0",
  "main": "index.js",
  "scripts": {
    "test": "echo \"Error: no test specified\" && exit 1",
    "wdio": "wdio run ./wdio.conf.ts"
  },
  "keywords": [],
  "author": "",
  "license": "ISC",
  "description": "",
  "devDependencies": {
    "@wdio/appium-service": "^9.11.0",
    "@wdio/cli": "^9.11.0",
    "@wdio/local-runner": "^9.11.0",
    "@wdio/mocha-framework": "^9.11.0",
    "@wdio/spec-reporter": "^9.11.0",
    "appium-uiautomator2-driver": "^4.1.1",
    "appium-xcuitest-driver": "^8.4.2",
    "chai": "^5.2.0",
    "webdriverio": "^9.11.0",
    "appium": "^2.17.0",
  }
}
```

The scripts section includes a command to run tests using WebdriverIO.
Dependencies include WebdriverIO, Appium service, Mocha, and Chai for assertions.

5. `tsconfig.json`—TypeScript Configuration (Optional)

If you are using **TypeScript** with WebdriverIO, this file helps configure TypeScript support.

It ensures **TypeScript** is properly compiled before running WebdriverIO tests. If not using TypeScript, this file is not required.

6. `package-lock.json`—Dependency Lock File

This file records the exact versions of installed packages.

- It helps maintain consistency across different environments.
- You don't need to modify this manually.

Now that our WebdriverIO project is set up, we have a clear structure in place. The next step is to write and execute tests. This setup ensures that all required configurations, dependencies, and test files are organized, making it easier to develop and maintain Appium automation scripts.

Creating Separate wdio.config.ts Files for Android and iOS

To efficiently manage **Android and iOS** test configurations in WebdriverIO, we should create separate configuration files for each platform. This allows us to customize capabilities and settings without modifying a single wdio.conf.ts file repeatedly.

1. Creating a common configuration file (wdio.conf.ts).

```
import { Options } from '@wdio/types'
export const config: Options.TestRunner = {
    runner: 'local',
    specs: ['./test/specs/**/*.ts'],
    maxInstances: 1,
    logLevel: 'info',
    framework: 'mocha',
    reporters: ['spec'],
    services: ['appium'],
    port: 4723,
    waitforTimeout: 10000,
```

CHAPTER 6   WRITING FIRST TEST

```
        mochaOpts: {
            timeout: 60000
        }
    };
```

   2. Creating wdio.android.conf.ts.

```
import { config as baseConfig } from './wdio.conf';
export const config = {
    ...baseConfig,
    capabilities: [
        {
            platformName: 'Android',
            'appium:deviceName': 'emulator-5554',
            'appium:platformVersion': '13.0',
            'appium:automationName': 'UiAutomator2',
            'appium:app': '/path/to/android/app.apk',
            'appium:autoGrantPermissions': true
        }
    ],
};
```

   3. Creating wdio.ios.conf.ts.

```
import { config as baseConfig } from './wdio.conf';
export const config = {
    ...baseConfig,
    capabilities: [
        {
            platformName: 'iOS',
            'appium:deviceName': 'iPhone 14',
            'appium:platformVersion': '16.0',
            'appium:automationName': 'XCUITest',
            'appium:app': '/path/to/ios/app.app'
        }
    ]};
```

101

CHAPTER 6   WRITING FIRST TEST

4. Since we are now starting the Appium server programmatically using the Appium service, it's crucial to capture and store the server logs in a file for effective debugging in case of failures.

```
services: [
    [
        'appium',
        {
            logPath: './logs',
            args: {
                log: './logs/appium.log'
            }
        }
    ]
]
```

5. Update the scripts section in package.json with the command to run android and iOS test.

```
"scripts": {
    "android": "wdio run ./wdio.android.conf.ts",
    "ios": "wdio run ./wdio.ios.conf.ts"
}
```

Now that we've created our first test, we still face a challenge. The locators for Android and iOS can vary depending on the chosen strategy. To maintain a single test while ensuring the correct locators are loaded based on the platform, we can introduce a class called `CustomCommands`. This class will override WDIO's $ and $$ methods, which correspond to `findElement` and `findElements`.

```
const platformKeyMap = {
android: 'android',
ios: 'ios',
};
browser.overwriteCommand('$', ($, selector) => {
let element = undefined;
if (typeof selector === 'string') {
element = $(selector);
```

CHAPTER 6   WRITING FIRST TEST

```
} else {
element = $(getSelectorByPlatform(selector));
}
return element;
});
browser.overwriteCommand('$$', ($$, selector) => {
let element = undefined;
if (typeof selector === 'string') {
element = $$(selector);
} else {
element = $$(getSelectorByPlatform(selector));
}
return element;
});
/**
 * Gets platform specfic selector.
 * @param {*} selector
 * @return {string} Platform specific selector.
 */
function getSelectorByPlatform(selector) {
const platform = getPlatform();
const platformKey = validateAndGetPlatformKey(platform);
return selector[platformKey];
}
/**
 * Gets current platform.
 * @return {string} platform
 */
function getPlatform() {
if (!driver.isMobile) return 'web';
return driver.isIOS ? 'ios' : 'android';
}
/**
 * Checks if platform specific selector set.
 * @param {string} platform
```

CHAPTER 6 WRITING FIRST TEST

```
 * @return {string} key
 */
function validateAndGetPlatformKey(platform) {
const platformKey = platformKeyMap[platform];
if (!platformKey) {
throw new Error(`Selector not set for ${platform} platform.`);
}
return platformKey;
}
```

This code customizes WDIO's $ and $$ commands to handle platform-specific locators dynamically. Instead of writing separate tests for Android and iOS, it allows a single test to work across both platforms by selecting the appropriate locator based on the platform. When a selector is passed as an object containing both `android` and `ios` keys, the script determines the current platform using `getPlatform()` and retrieves the corresponding locator using `getSelectorByPlatform()`. If the test is running on Android, the `android` locator is used, and if on iOS, the `ios` locator is used. Such an approach eliminates the need for platform-specific conditions in test scripts, making them cleaner and more maintainable. Additionally, the `validateAndGetPlatformKey()` function ensures that a valid platform key exists, preventing potential errors due to missing selectors.

For Android, because the element does not expose any faster lookup strategy such as ID or accessibility ID, we are forced to use xpath, which is not recommended; however, if no other locators can be found, you can consider xpath.

Locators will look like

```
const selectors = {
loginButton:
{     android: '//android.widget.TextView[@text="Login"]',
      ios: -ios predicate string:name == "Login", },
};
export default selectors;
```

This code defines an object called `selectors` that stores platform-specific locators for different UI elements. In this case, it includes a `loginButton` selector with separate xpath for Android (`//android.widget.TextView[@text="Login"]`) and an iOS-specific locator using **iOS Predicate String** (`-ios predicate string:name == "Login"`). By exporting `selectors`, this object can be imported and used in test scripts to dynamically fetch the correct locator based on the platform, ensuring a single, maintainable test for both Android and iOS.

Now the test code will look as below.

```
import { expect } from 'chai';
import LoginLocators from './locators';
describe('First Appium Test', () => {
it('should launch the app and verify an element', async () => {
const loginButton = $(LoginLocators.loginButton);
expect(await loginButton.isDisplayed()).to.be.true;
});
});
```

Summary

Now that our WebdriverIO project is set up, we have a clear structure in place. The next step is to write and execute tests. This setup ensures that all required configurations, dependencies, and test files are organized, making it easier to develop and maintain Appium automation scripts.

To enhance reusability and maintainability, we have also implemented a platform-aware locator strategy. By overriding WDIO's $ and $$ commands, we ensure that platform-specific locators are selected dynamically based on whether the test is running on Android or iOS. Instead of using conditional logic in test scripts, our custom implementation fetches the correct locator automatically using a structured `selectors` object. This eliminates code duplication, making the test scripts cleaner and more efficient.

With this setup, our test suite remains scalable, allowing us to write a single test that adapts to different platforms without additional modifications.

CHAPTER 7

Understand Appium Logs

What Will You Learn

In this chapter, you will learn how to interpret Appium logs, understand where logs originate from within the server, and debug test failures efficiently. You will explore different log sources within Appium; learn the structure of Appium logs; troubleshoot common server, driver, and session-related issues; and apply practical debugging techniques to resolve test failures.

Introduction to Appium Server Logs

Appium server logs are an essential tool for debugging and troubleshooting mobile automation tests. They provide insights into server operations, driver behavior, and communication between the Appium server, client, and connected devices. Understanding these logs helps in diagnosing failures, identifying performance bottlenecks, and ensuring smooth automation runs.

Breaking Down the Android Logs

Structure of Appium Logs

Appium logs follow a structured format that includes

- **Timestamps:** Indicating when each log entry was recorded.
- **Log Levels:** Such as INFO, DEBUG, WARN, and ERROR, which indicate the severity of messages.
- **Modules:** Logs are categorized based on their source (e.g., [Appium], [HTTP], [ADB], [AndroidUiautomator2Driver]).

Identifying Key Modules

1. **[Appium]**: General Appium server messages, including startup details.
2. **[HTTP]**: HTTP request and response logs showing interactions between client and server.
3. **[AppiumDriver]**: These are logs from the umbrella driver. This driver is responsible for session management and request routing. Every driver and plugin has their own logger instance.
4. **[AndroidUiautomator2Driver]**: Logs specific to the UiAutomator2 driver.
5. **[ADB]**: Messages related to Android Debug Bridge (ADB) commands which reside inside the appium-adb module.
6. **[Logcat]**: Captured Android system logs.

Understanding Appium Server Startup Logs

Let's break down the Appium server logs step by step to understand what happens when the server starts.

Server Initialization

```
2025-03-14 03:53:30:922 [Appium] Welcome to Appium v2.17.0
```

This log indicates that the Appium server has started, and the version being used is 2.17.0.

Server Arguments and Configuration

```
2025-03-14 03:53:30:923 [Appium] Non-default server args:
2025-03-14 03:53:30:924 [Appium] { basePath: '/wd/hub' }
```

These lines show that the Appium server was started with specific nondefault arguments. The `basePath` is set to /wd/hub, which means all API requests will be accessible from the root path.

Appium Home Path Detection

2025-03-14 03:53:30:924 [Appium] The autodetected Appium home path: /Users/saikrishna/Documents/Book/ch-6/wdio-appium-project

If the home path is not explicitly specified as a command-line argument or an environment variable, the Appium server will determine it automatically.

Driver Loading

2025-03-14 03:53:30:924 [Appium] Attempting to load driver uiautomator2...
2025-03-14 03:53:30:925 [Appium] Requiring driver at /Users/saikrishna/Documents/Book/ch-6/wdio-appium-project/node_modules/appium-uiautomator2-driver/build/index.js
2025-03-14 03:53:31:537 [Appium] AndroidUiautomator2Driver has been successfully loaded in 0.612s

These logs indicate that Appium is loading the UiAutomator2 driver, which is required for automating Android devices. The driver is located in the specified path, and it has been successfully loaded in 0.612 seconds.

HTTP Interface Initialization

2025-03-14 03:53:31:545 [Appium] Appium REST http interface listener started on http://0.0.0.0:4723

The Appium server starts listening for incoming HTTP requests on port 4723. The 0.0.0.0 address means it can accept connections from any network interface.

Available Connection URLs

This information will assist users in properly configuring their clients.

2025-03-14 03:53:31:546 [Appium] You can provide the following URLs in your client code to connect to this server:

http://127.0.0.1:4723/ (only accessible from the same host)
http://192.168.29.249:4723/
http://10.255.0.7:4723/

CHAPTER 7   UNDERSTAND APPIUM LOGS

These are the available URLs that can be used to connect to the Appium server. The 127.0.0.1 address is for local connections, while the others are network-accessible.

Installed Drivers and Plugins

```
2025-03-14 03:53:31:546 [Appium] Available drivers:
2025-03-14 03:53:31:546 [Appium]   - uiautomator2@4.1.1 (automationName 'UiAutomator2')
2025-03-14 03:53:31:546 [Appium] No plugins have been installed. Use the "appium plugin" command to install the one(s) you want to use.
```

The Appium server lists installed drivers and plugins. Here, the UiAutomator2 driver (version 4.1.1) is available, and no plugins are installed.

Session Creation and Capabilities Handling

After the server starts, the next step is session creation when a test script is executed. Below is a breakdown of the logs during session initialization.

Incoming Session Request

```
2025-03-14 03:53:32:010 [HTTP] --> POST /session {"capabilities":{"alwaysMatch":{"platformName":"Android","appium:automationName":"UiAutomator2","appium:app":"https://github.com/webdriverio/native-demo-app/releases/download/v1.0.8/android.wdio.native.app.v1.0.8.apk","appium:autoGrantPermissions":true},"firstMatch":[{}]}}
```

This log indicates that a new session request is being sent to the Appium server via an HTTP POST /session request. The test script specifies capabilities such as platformName: Android, automationName: UiAutomator2, and app URL.

Processing the Session Request

```
2025-03-14 03:53:32:011 [AppiumDriver@6378] Calling AppiumDriver.createSession() with args: [null,null,{...}]
```

This log shows that Appium is attempting to create a new session based on the provided capabilities.

Matching the Requested Driver

2025-03-14 03:53:32:013 [Appium] Attempting to find matching driver for automationName 'UiAutomator2' and platformName 'Android'
2025-03-14 03:53:32:013 [Appium] The 'uiautomator2' driver was installed and matched caps.

Appium verifies that the requested driver (UiAutomator2) is installed and can handle the given capabilities.

Initializing the Driver

2025-03-14 03:53:32:015 [AppiumDriver@6378] Appium v2.17.0 creating new AndroidUiautomator2Driver (v4.1.1) session

The AndroidUiautomator2Driver (version 4.1.1) is initialized for the session.

Finalizing the Session Creation

2025-03-14 03:53:32:021 [12228f40][AndroidUiautomator2Driver@437e] Session created with session id: 12228f40-e7f5-4c58-ab78-e08db6536c4f

This log confirms that the session has been successfully created and assigned a unique session ID (12228f40-e7f5-4c58-ab78-e08db6536c4f). This session ID will be referenced in subsequent logs when executing commands.

ADB Initialization and Device Detection

Once the session is created, Appium ensures that ADB is correctly set up and detects available Android devices.

2025-03-14 03:53:32:027 [12228f40][ADB] Found 3 'build-tools' folders under '/Users/saikrishna/Library/Android/sdk' (newest first):
2025-03-14 03:53:32:027 [12228f40][ADB]   /Users/saikrishna/Library/Android/sdk/build-tools/35.0.0
2025-03-14 03:53:32:027 [12228f40][ADB]   /Users/saikrishna/Library/Android/sdk/build-tools/34.0.0
2025-03-14 03:53:32:027 [12228f40][ADB]   /Users/saikrishna/Library/Android/sdk/build-tools/30.0.3

CHAPTER 7 UNDERSTAND APPIUM LOGS

This log entry shows that Appium has detected multiple versions of Android build tools. The most recent version (35.0.0) is typically used unless specified otherwise.

Starting ADB Server

```
2025-03-14 03:53:32:027 [12228f40][ADB] Using 'adb' from '/Users/
saikrishna/Library/Android/sdk/platform-tools/adb'
2025-03-14 03:53:32:027 [12228f40][ADB] Running '/Users/saikrishna/Library/
Android/sdk/platform-tools/adb -P 5037 start-server'
```

These logs indicate that Appium is using ADB from the specified directory and starting the ADB server.

Retrieving Connected Devices

```
2025-03-14 03:53:32:048 [12228f40][AndroidUiautomator2Driver@437e]
Retrieving device list
2025-03-14 03:53:32:048 [12228f40][ADB] Trying to find connected
Android devices
2025-03-14 03:53:32:049 [12228f40][ADB] Getting connected devices
```

Appium queries ADB to list all connected Android devices.

Detecting an Active Emulator

```
2025-03-14 03:53:32:063 [12228f40][ADB] Connected devices: [{"udid":"emulator-
5554","state":"device"}]
```

Here, Appium detects an active emulator (emulator-5554) that is in a device state, meaning it is ready for automation.

Post this appium will install the settings application and also the application under test. Once these steps are done. Appium server is only responsible for managing extensions and routing. It listens as HTTP/WebSocket server and provides the foundation for multiple extensions to perform automation for their destination platforms using WebDriver API protocols.

Starting UiAutomator2 Server on the Device

Once a device is detected, Appium starts the UiAutomator2 server inside the Android device which is located inside appium-uiautomator2-server and the package is designed as native Android integration test, whose main task is to open an HTTP server on the destination device and enables communication between the driver and the server inside the device.

Launching UiAutomator2 Instrumentation

2025-03-14 03:53:38:088 [12228f40][ADB] Creating ADB subprocess with args: ["-P","5037","-s","emulator-5554","shell","am","instrument","-w","-e", "disableAnalytics","true","io.appium.uiautomator2.server.test/androidx. test.runner.AndroidJUnitRunner"]

This log shows that Appium is launching the UiAutomator2 instrumentation process on the emulator (emulator-5554). The AndroidJUnitRunner is responsible for executing the tests inside the device.

Checking UiAutomator2 Server Status

2025-03-14 03:53:38:091 [12228f40][AndroidUiautomator2Driver@437e] Matched '/status' to command name 'getStatus'
2025-03-14 03:53:38:092 [12228f40][AndroidUiautomator2Driver@437e] Proxying [GET /status] to [GET http://127.0.0.1:8201/status] with no body

After starting UiAutomator2, Appium repeatedly checks whether the server is ready by sending status requests to http://127.0.0.1:8201/status.

Handling Initial Connection Delays

2025-03-14 03:53:38:108 [12228f40][AndroidUiautomator2Driver@437e] socket hang up

The socket hang up messages indicate that the UiAutomator2 server is not yet ready. This is normal as the server takes a few seconds to initialize.

Confirmation of UiAutomator2 Server Readiness

```
2025-03-14 03:53:41:156 [12228f40][AndroidUiautomator2Driver@437e] Got
response with status 200: {"sessionId":"None","value":{"message":"UiAutomat
or2 Server is ready to accept commands","ready":true}}
```

After a few retries, the server responds with status 200, confirming that UiAutomator2 is now ready to accept commands.

Establishing a New Session on the Device

```
2025-03-14 03:53:41:157 [12228f40][AndroidUiautomator2Driver@437e] Proxying
[POST /session] to [POST http://127.0.0.1:8201/session] with body: {...}
```

At this point, Appium forwards the session creation request to the UiAutomator2 server, passing all required capabilities.

Final Session Confirmation

```
2025-03-14 03:53:41:167 [12228f40][AndroidUiautomator2Driver@437e] Got
response with status 200: {"sessionId":"5a74a76c-a52f-4123-9552-
9e025870b766","value":{...}}
```

The session is successfully created inside the device, and UiAutomator2 is now fully operational.

Handling Appium Client Commands

Once the UiAutomator2 session is created, Appium client commands are passed to the `appium-uiautomator2-driver`, which proxies them to the UiAutomator2 server running inside the device.

Finding an Element Using XPath

2025-03-14 03:53:42:533 [12228f40][HTTP] --> POST /session/12228f40-e7f5-4c58-ab78-e08db6536c4f/element {"using":"xpath","value":"//android.widget.TextView[@text=\"Login\"]"}

This log shows that the Appium client has sent a request to find an element with the XPath //android.widget.TextView[@text="Login"] within the active session.

Processing the Find Element Request

2025-03-14 03:53:42:535 [12228f40][AndroidUiautomator2Driver@437e] Calling AppiumDriver.findElement() with args: ["xpath","//android.widget.TextView[@text=\"Login\"]","12228f40-e7f5-4c58-ab78-e08db6536c4f"]

The AndroidUiautomator2Driver receives the request and attempts to find the element using the specified XPath.

Valid Locator Strategies

2025-03-14 03:53:42:536 [12228f40][AndroidUiautomator2Driver@437e] Valid locator strategies for this request: xpath, id, class name, accessibility id, css selector, -android uiautomator

This log confirms the supported locator strategies that can be used to find elements.

Proxying the Request to UiAutomator2 Server

2025-03-14 03:53:42:538 [12228f40][AndroidUiautomator2Driver@437e] Proxying [POST /element] to [POST http://127.0.0.1:8201/session/5a74a76c-a52f-4123-9552-9e025870b766/element] with body: {"strategy":"xpath","selector":"//android.widget.TextView[@text=\"Login\"]","context":"","multiple":false}

The request is forwarded to the UiAutomator2 server inside the device for processing.

Element Found Successfully

```
2025-03-14 03:53:43:885 [12228f40][AndroidUiautomator2Driver@437e] Got
response with status 200: {"sessionId":"5a74a76c-a52f-4123-95
52-9e025870b766","value":{"ELEMENT":"00000000-0000-0048-ffff-
ffff00000033","element-6066-11e4-a52e-4f735466cecf":"00000000-0000-0048-
ffff-ffff00000033"}}
```

The element has been successfully found, and its unique identifier (ELEMENT: 00000000-0000-0048-ffff-ffff00000033) is returned to the client.

Returning the Element to the Client

```
2025-03-14 03:53:43:886 [12228f40][AndroidUiautomator2Driver@437e]
Responding to client with driver.findElement() result: {"element-6066-11e4-
a52e-4f735466cecf":"00000000-0000-0048-ffff-ffff00000033","ELEMENT":
"00000000-0000-0048-ffff-ffff00000033"}
```

The element is returned to the Appium client, completing the findElement command successfully.

Understanding iOS Server Logs

Now that we have explored the Android logs, let's shift our focus to iOS. Appium interacts with iOS devices using the XCUITest driver, which relies on WebDriverAgent (WDA) to execute commands on real devices and simulators. Understanding the iOS logs is crucial for diagnosing issues related to server startup, session creation, and command execution. In this chapter, we will analyze step-by-step logs to understand how Appium initializes and manages iOS sessions.

iOS Server Initialization

Before Appium can interact with an iOS device, it initializes the server and loads the necessary drivers. Let's analyze the logs to understand how Appium prepares for iOS automation.

CHAPTER 7 UNDERSTAND APPIUM LOGS

Server Startup

2025-03-14 06:57:05:715 [Appium] Welcome to Appium v2.17.0

This confirms that the Appium server has successfully started, using version 2.17.0.

Server Configuration and Home Path Detection

2025-03-14 06:57:05:716 [Appium] Non-default server args:
2025-03-14 06:57:05:716 [Appium] { basePath: '/' }
2025-03-14 06:57:05:716 [Appium] The autodetected Appium home path: /Users/saikrishna/Documents/Book/ch-6/wdio-appium-project

Appium detects its home path and ensures it is set up correctly for running tests.

Loading Required Drivers

2025-03-14 06:57:05:717 [Appium] Attempting to load driver uiautomator2...
2025-03-14 06:57:05:717 [Appium] Attempting to load driver xcuitest...

Here, Appium attempts to load both Android (UiAutomator2) and iOS (XCUITest) drivers, ensuring that tests for both platforms can be executed.

Verifying Driver Installation

2025-03-14 06:57:06:266 [Appium] XCUITestDriver has been successfully loaded in 0.549s

This confirms that the XCUITest driver has been successfully loaded, meaning the necessary dependencies are in place for iOS automation.

Appium Server Listening for Commands

2025-03-14 06:57:06:756 [Appium] Appium REST http interface listener started on http://0.0.0.0:4723

Appium is now listening for incoming automation requests on port 4723, making it ready to accept commands.

CHAPTER 7   UNDERSTAND APPIUM LOGS

Available Drivers and Plugins

```
2025-03-14 06:57:06:756 [Appium] Available drivers:
2025-03-14 06:57:06:756 [Appium]    - uiautomator2@4.1.1 (automationName 'UiAutomator2')
2025-03-14 06:57:06:756 [Appium]    - xcuitest@8.4.2 (automationName 'XCUITest')
```

The Appium server lists all installed drivers, confirming that both UiAutomator2 and XCUITest are available.

Next, we will analyze how Appium initiates a session on an iOS device using WebDriverAgent.

iOS Session Creation and Capability Handling

Once the Appium server is running, the next step is creating a session for iOS automation. Let's analyze the logs to understand the session creation process.

Incoming Session Request

```
2025-03-14 06:57:07:250 [HTTP] --> POST /session {"capabilities":{"alwaysMatch":{"platformName":"iOS","appium:automationName":"XCUITest","appium:app":"https://github.com/webdriverio/native-demo-app/releases/download/v1.0.8/ios.simulator.wdio.native.app.v1.0.8.zip"},"firstMatch":[{}]}}
```

This log indicates that an Appium client has sent a request to start a new session with the XCUITest driver for iOS. The test specifies capabilities such as platformName: iOS, automationName: XCUITest, and the application URL.

Processing the Session Request

```
2025-03-14 06:57:07:250 [AppiumDriver@5029] Calling AppiumDriver.createSession() with args: [...]
```

Appium begins processing the session request by calling the createSession function.

Matching the Requested Driver

2025-03-14 06:57:07:252 [Appium] Attempting to find matching driver for automationName 'XCUITest' and platformName 'iOS'
2025-03-14 06:57:07:252 [Appium] The 'xcuitest' driver was installed and matched caps.

The server verifies that the requested driver (XCUITest) is installed and supports the provided capabilities.

Initializing the XCUITest Driver

2025-03-14 06:57:07:253 [AppiumDriver@5029] Appium v2.17.0 creating new XCUITestDriver (v8.4.2) session

The XCUITestDriver (version 8.4.2) is initialized to handle the iOS session.

Checking BaseDriver Compatibility

2025-03-14 06:57:07:253 [AppiumDriver@5029] Checking BaseDriver versions for Appium and XCUITestDriver
2025-03-14 06:57:07:253 [AppiumDriver@5029] Appium's BaseDriver version is 9.16.3
2025-03-14 06:57:07:253 [AppiumDriver@5029] XCUITestDriver's BaseDriver version is 9.16.3

Appium confirms that both the core BaseDriver and XCUITestDriver are compatible.

Creating the Session with Capabilities

2025-03-14 06:57:07:255 [XCUITestDriver@ad5f] Creating session with W3C capabilities: {...}

This log confirms that a session is being created using the WebDriver W3C standard capabilities.

Missing Platform Version Warning

2025-03-14 06:57:07:257 [XCUITestDriver@ad5f] 'platformVersion' capability ('undefined') is not a valid version number. Consider fixing it or be ready to experience inconsistent driver behavior.

A warning is logged because the platformVersion capability was not provided. While the session may still start, this can cause instability.

So, when running tests on simulator, if the deviceName and platformVersion are not specified, Appium will first look for any simulators that have already booted and select that simulator for test execution, which may not be the simulator the user wishes to test on. That's why it is crucial to be explicit about the deviceName and its platform.

If the UDID capability is given, then Appium will check if the UDID belongs to a simulator or real device and take next action based on that.

Finalizing the Session Creation

```
2025-03-14 06:57:07:257 [bb3c9915][XCUITestDriver@ad5f] Session created
with session id: bb3c9915-7626-484e-b868-2f5ca6f136d9
```

The session is successfully created and assigned a unique session ID (bb3c9915-7626-484e-b868-2f5ca6f136d9). This ID will be referenced in subsequent logs when executing commands on the iOS device.

Now Appium will work on the application under test installation process and build WDA on simulator/device.

Next, we will analyze how WebDriverAgent (WDA) is initialized to communicate with the iOS device/simulator.

Initializing WebDriverAgent (WDA)

Once the iOS session is created, Appium initializes WebDriverAgent (WDA), which facilitates communication between Appium and the iOS device.

Requesting Device Connection

```
2025-03-14 06:57:21:492 [bb3c9915][DevCon Factory] Requesting connection
for device DA499F7B-468E-4C0C-9A2C-60F8460AFEB2 on local port 8100
```

Appium attempts to establish a connection with the iOS device via port 8100, which is used for WDA communication. This process is slightly more sophisticated than local communication. The driver doesn't talk to the iOS device directly; instead, it communicates with **WebDriverAgent (WDA)**, a server running on the device itself. WDA acts as a separate network entity. To facilitate seamless communication with WDA, we need to forward its port to the host machine where the Appium server is running.

This step is essential because it allows the Appium server to interact with WDA transparently, without needing to know the device's actual IP address or subnet. Once port forwarding is established, similar to the mechanism used in Android, we can communicate with WDA as if it were part of the local network, abstracting away the device's underlying physical network configuration.

Checking WDA Status

2025-03-14 06:57:21:497 [bb3c9915][WD Proxy] Proxying [GET /status] to [GET http://127.0.0.1:8100/status] with no body

XCUITest driver queries the status of WDA to check if it is running on the simulator/device.

WDA Upgrade and Reinstallation

2025-03-14 06:57:21:510 [bb3c9915][XCUITestDriver@ad5f] Will uninstall running WDA since it has different version in comparison to the one which is bundled with appium-xcuitest-driver module (1741932553950 != 1741083476684)

Appium detects that the WDA version on the device is outdated, so it uninstalls the existing WDA and prepares to reinstall it.

Starting WebDriverAgent

2025-03-14 06:57:21:835 [bb3c9915][XCUITestDriver@ad5f] Trying to start WebDriverAgent 2 times with 10000ms interval
2025-03-14 06:57:21:838 [bb3c9915][XCUITestDriver@ad5f] Launching WebDriverAgent on the device

WDA is now being launched on the iOS device.

Running WebDriverAgent with Xcode

2025-03-14 06:57:22:590 [bb3c9915][XCUITestDriver@ad5f] Beginning test with command 'xcodebuild build-for-testing test-without-building -project /Users/saikrishna/Documents/Book/ch-6/wdio-appium-project/node_modules/appium-xcuitest-driver/node_modules/appium-webdriveragent/WebDriverAgent.xcodeproj -scheme WebDriverAgentRunner'

CHAPTER 7   UNDERSTAND APPIUM LOGS

Appium compiles and launches WDA using Xcode to enable automation on the device, which enforces strict code signing and app deployment requirements. Unlike Android, where a test server can be pushed via ADB without compilation, iOS mandates that any app (including WDA) be signed with a valid development certificate and provisioned for the target device.

By compiling WDA through Xcode, Appium ensures that the server is properly signed and installed on the device, enabling it to run in compliance with Apple's security policies. Once launched, WDA listens for automation commands and acts as the bridge between the Appium server and the iOS device.

Waiting for WDA to Start

```
2025-03-14 06:57:23:811 [bb3c9915][XCUITestDriver@ad5f] Waiting up to
60000ms for WebDriverAgent to start
2025-03-14 06:57:23:811 [bb3c9915][XCUITestDriver@ad5f] Proxying [GET /
status] to [GET http://127.0.0.1:8100/status] with no body
```

Appium repeatedly checks the WDA status while waiting for it to start.

Handling WDA Connection Issues

```
2025-03-14 06:57:23:844 [bb3c9915][XCUITestDriver@ad5f] connect
ECONNREFUSED 127.0.0.1:8100
```

This log indicates that Appium is trying to communicate with WDA, but the connection is being refused. This may happen if WDA is not fully initialized yet.

Appium will continue retrying until WDA successfully starts and is ready to accept commands.

WebDriverAgent Successfully Started

```
2025-03-14 06:58:01:076 [bb3c9915][XCUITestDriver@ad5f] Got response with
status 200: {"value":{"build":{"upgradedAt":"1741932553950","version":"9.1.
0","time":"Mar 14 2025 12:27:45","productBundleIdentifier":"com.facebook.We
bDriverAgentRunner"},"os":{"testmanagerdVersion":65535,"name":"iOS","sdkVer
sion":"18.0","version":"18.2"},"device":"iphone","ios":{"simulatorVersion"
:"18.2","ip":"192.168.29.249"},"message":"WebDriverAgent is ready to accept
commands","state":"success","ready":true},"sessionId":null}
```

CHAPTER 7   UNDERSTAND APPIUM LOGS

This log confirms that WebDriverAgent (WDA) has successfully started and is now ready to accept automation commands.

Creating a New WebDriverAgent Session

```
2025-03-14 06:58:01:078 [bb3c9915][XCUITestDriver@ad5f] Sending
createSession command to WDA
```

Appium sends a request to WDA to create a new session for executing automation commands.

```
2025-03-14 06:58:01:082 [bb3c9915][XCUITestDriver@ad5f] Proxying [POST
/session] to [POST http://127.0.0.1:8100/session] with body:
{"capabilities":{"firstMatch":[{"bundleId":"org.reactjs.native.example.
wdiodemoapp","arguments":[],"environment":{},"eventloopIdleDelaySec":0,
"shouldWaitForQuiescence":true,"shouldUseTestManagerForVisibilityDetection"
:false,"maxTypingFrequency":60,"shouldUseSingletonTestManager":true,
"shouldTerminateApp":true,"forceAppLaunch":true,"useNativeCachingStrategy":
true,"forceSimulatorSoftwareKeyboardPresence":true}],"alwaysMatch":{}}}
```

This request includes important session capabilities, such as `bundleId` (to launch the correct app), `shouldWaitForQuiescence`, and `forceAppLaunch`.

Successful Session Creation

```
2025-03-14 06:58:03:409 [bb3c9915][XCUITestDriver@ad5f] Got response with
status 200: {"value":{"sessionId":"8D8C1D96-FBB6-4C7D-8753-05E34AEED83F",
"capabilities":{"sdkVersion":"18.2","device":"iphone"}},"sessionId":
"8D8C1D96-FBB6-4C7D-8753-05E34AEED83F"}
```

The session has been successfully created, and WDA assigns a unique session ID (8D8C1D96-FBB6-4C7D-8753-05E34AEED83F). This session ID will be referenced in subsequent automation commands.

Handling Appium Client Commands

Once the WDA session is created, Appium client commands are sent to the `appium-xcuitest-driver`, which then proxies them to the WebDriverAgent running on the iOS device.

CHAPTER 7 UNDERSTAND APPIUM LOGS

Finding an Element Using Predicate String

```
2025-03-14 06:58:03:455 [bb3c9915][HTTP] --> POST /session/bb3c9915-
7626-484e-b868-2f5ca6f136d9/element {"using":"-ios predicate string",
"value":"name == \"Login\""}
```

This log shows that the Appium client has sent a request to find an element using the iOS predicate string strategy with the condition name == "Login".

Processing the Find Element Request

```
2025-03-14 06:58:03:456 [bb3c9915][XCUITestDriver@ad5f] Calling
AppiumDriver.findElement() with args: ["-ios predicate string",
"name == \"Login\"","bb3c9915-7626-484e-b868-2f5ca6f136d9"]
```

You might notice a suffix like [bb3c9915][XCUITestDriver@ad5f] appearing in Appium logs. This suffix is helpful for identifying and distinguishing between multiple instances of the same driver, which is especially useful when running parallel tests. The part after the @ (e.g., ad5f) acts as a unique identifier for that specific driver instance.

When managing multiple sessions, ensuring each driver instance has a unique suffix helps with debugging, log tracing, and overall test stability.

The XCUITestDriver receives the request and attempts to locate the element.

Valid Locator Strategies

```
2025-03-14 06:58:03:456 [bb3c9915][XCUITestDriver@ad5f] Valid locator
strategies for this request: xpath, id, name, class name, -ios predicate
string, -ios class chain, accessibility id, css selector
```

This log confirms that multiple locator strategies are available, and -ios predicate string is a valid choice for finding elements.

Proxying the Request to WebDriverAgent

```
2025-03-14 06:58:03:460 [bb3c9915][XCUITestDriver@ad5f] Proxying
[POST /element] to [POST http://127.0.0.1:8100/session/8D8C1D96-
FBB6-4C7D-8753-05E34AEED83F/element] with body: {"using":"predicate
string","value":"name == \"Login\""}
```

The request is forwarded to the WebDriverAgent server inside the iOS device.

Element Found Successfully

```
2025-03-14 06:58:03:562 [bb3c9915][XCUITestDriver@ad5f] Got response with
status 200: {"value":{"ELEMENT":"16000000-0000-0000-140F-010000000000",
"element-6066-11e4-a52e-4f735466cecf":"16000000-0000-0000-140F-01000000
0000"},"sessionId":"8D8C1D96-FBB6-4C7D-8753-05E34AEED83F"}
```

The element has been successfully located, and its unique identifier (ELEMENT: 16000000-0000-0000-140F-010000000000) is returned to the client, completing the findElement command successfully.

Summary

In this chapter, we explored how to interpret Appium server logs for both Android and iOS automation. We broke down the server initialization process, session creation, and communication between Appium, its drivers, and mobile devices.

For Android, we analyzed how Appium loads the UiAutomator2 driver, detects connected devices using ADB, and starts the UiAutomator2 server. We also walked through how Appium proxies automation commands to the device and retrieves element information.

For iOS, we examined how Appium initializes the XCUITest driver, launches WebDriverAgent (WDA), and establishes a session. We looked into WDA installation, session creation, and handling client commands through WebDriverAgent.

By understanding these logs, testers and developers can efficiently debug automation failures, identify issues with driver initialization, and troubleshoot session-related problems. Mastering Appium logs will help in ensuring smooth and reliable mobile test automation.

CHAPTER 8

All You Need to Know on Gestures

What We Will Learn

In this chapter, you will learn how to perform various gestures in mobile automation using Appium, with a focus on the modern and recommended approach, the W3C Actions API. You will understand how the Actions API works under the hood, including its use of input sources, action sequences, and tick-based timelines to simulate realistic user interactions.

WebDriver Specification: Actions API

The foundation for performing complex user interactions in modern automation frameworks like Appium lies in the WebDriver W3C Actions API, as defined in the official WebDriver Level 2 specification. This specification introduces a structured and standardized approach to simulating user interactions across multiple input modalities such as mouse, keyboard, touch, and pen. In the context of mobile automation, touch-based interactions are especially relevant. The Actions API is built around the idea of "input sources," where each source represents a virtual user (e.g., a finger on a touchscreen), and each one is associated with a series of discrete actions like pointerDown, pointerMove, and pointerUp. These actions are grouped into a timeline divided into "ticks," where each tick represents a simultaneous execution point for actions across input sources. This architecture allows for powerful, synchronized, and multitouch interactions such as pinch, zoom, swipe, and drag-and-drop. For mobile testers and developers, this specification ensures that gesture simulations are not only consistent across platforms and tools but also granular and flexible enough to reflect real-world usage patterns. Refer to Figure 8-1.

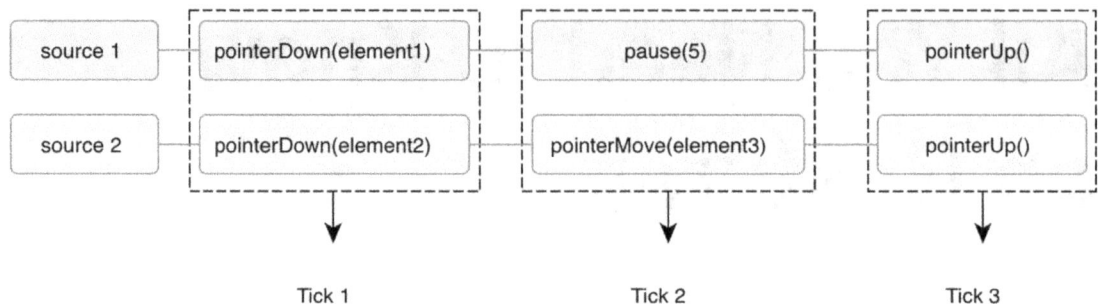

Figure 8-1. Actions API (https://www.w3.org/TR/webdriver2/#actions)

How to Perform a Gesture in Detail

Using Appium, gestures can be implemented in code by directly leveraging the W3C Actions API through the Appium client libraries (such as Java, Python, or JavaScript). To perform a gesture, the first step is to define an input source, typically a PointerInput of type TOUCH, which represents a virtual finger on the screen. Once the input source is defined, you construct a sequence of actions that map to the gesture you want to simulate. For instance, to simulate a swipe gesture, you would start by moving the finger to the starting position using pointerMove, then issue a pointerDown command to simulate touching the screen. After that, you would use another pointerMove to simulate the drag motion to the destination point and finally issue a pointerUp to lift the finger. These actions are added to a Sequence object, which is then passed to the WebDriver using the perform() method. The duration of each move can be customized to simulate fast or slow swipes, and multiple sequences can be used in tandem to simulate multitouch interactions like pinch or zoom. This low-level control enables precise reproduction of real user behavior, making the test scenarios more robust and accurate.

CHAPTER 8   ALL YOU NEED TO KNOW ON GESTURES

Interpreting the Gesture from the Image in Figure 8-2

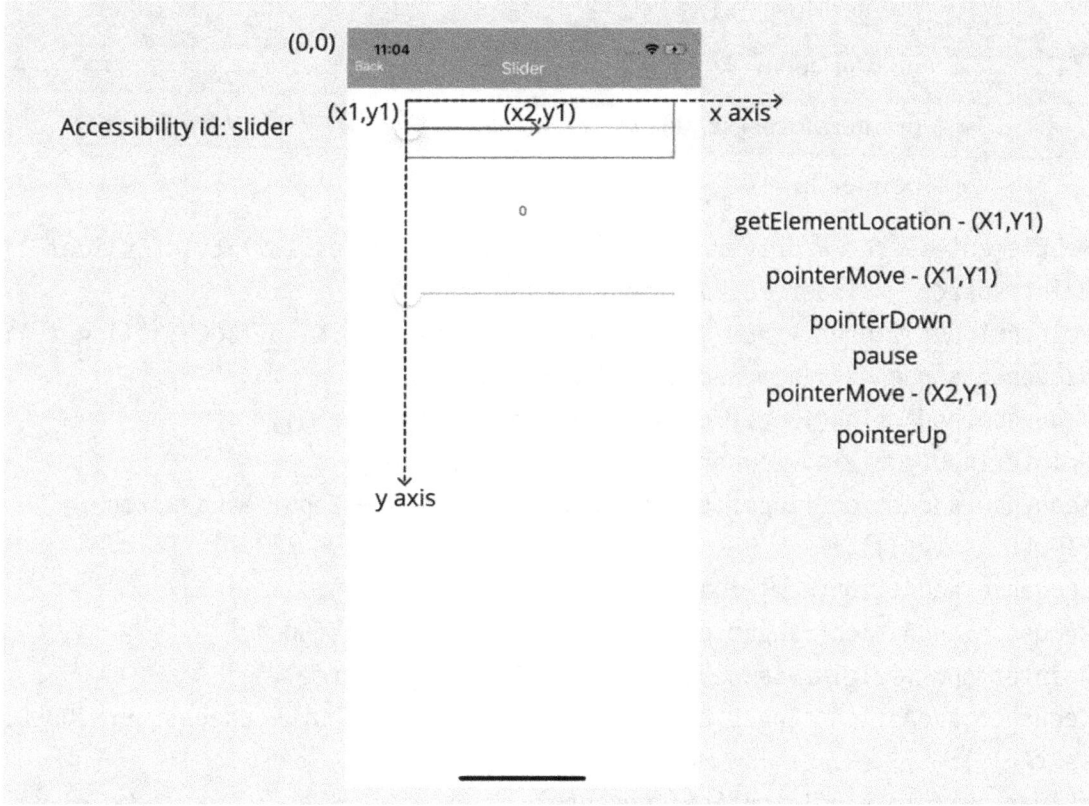

Figure 8-2. Swipe gesture

The image represents a **horizontal swipe gesture** performed on a slider UI element. The gesture starts at the left end of the slider ((x1, y1)) and moves rightward to (x2, y1), which remains on the same vertical axis (hence a purely horizontal movement). This mirrors what a user would do when adjusting a slider by dragging their finger across the screen.

Key elements shown:

- **Coordinate system** with origin (0,0) at the top left.

- The **element is** identified by **accessibility ID: slider**.

- A **pointer gesture path** from (x1, y1) to (x2, y1) representing the swipe.

CHAPTER 8   ALL YOU NEED TO KNOW ON GESTURES

- The **steps of the gesture** listed are
  - pointerMove–(x1,y1)
  - pointerDown
  - pointerMove–(x2,y1)
  - pointerUp

```
WebElement slider = driver.findElement(AppiumBy.accessibilityId("slider"));
Point source = slider.getLocation();
PointerInput finger = new PointerInput(PointerInput.Kind.TOUCH, "finger");
Sequence sequence = new Sequence(finger, 1);
sequence.addAction(finger.createPointerMove(ofMillis(0),
PointerInput.Origin.viewport(), source.x, source.y));
sequence.addAction(finger.createPointerDown(PointerInput.MouseButton.
MIDDLE.asArg()));
sequence.addAction(new Pause(finger, ofMillis(600)));
sequence.addAction(finger.createPointerMove(ofMillis(600),
PointerInput.Origin.viewport(), source.x + 400, source.y));
sequence.addAction(finger.createPointerUp(PointerInput.MouseButton.MIDDLE.
asArg()));
driver.perform(singletonList(sequence));
```

Step-by-Step Breakdown of the Code

```
WebElement slider = driver.findElement(AppiumBy.
accessibilityId("slider"));
Point source = slider.getLocation();
```

1. Locate the UI element using the accessibility ID "slider" and fetch its screen coordinates (x1, y1).

```
PointerInput finger = new PointerInput(PointerInput.Kind.TOUCH, "finger");
Sequence sequence = new Sequence(finger, 1);
```

2. Initialize the gesture with a virtual touch input named "finger" and create a sequence to store the actions.

```
sequence.addAction(finger.createPointerMove(ofMillis(0),
PointerInput.Origin.viewport(), source.x, source.y));
```

3. Move the finger to the starting point (x1, y1) instantly (0 ms delay).

```
sequence.addAction(finger.createPointerDown(PointerInput.MouseButton.
MIDDLE.asArg()));
```

4. Touch down at the starting point, simulating the user placing their finger on the screen.

```
sequence.addAction(new Pause(finger, ofMillis(600)));
```

5. Pause for 600 ms, mimicking a natural press-and-hold.

```
sequence.addAction(finger.createPointerMove(ofMillis(600),
PointerInput.Origin.viewport(), source.x + 400, source.y));
```

6. Move the finger horizontally to the right by 400 pixels over 600 ms, maintaining the same y coordinate.

```
sequence.addAction(finger.createPointerUp(PointerInput.MouseButton.MIDDLE.
asArg()));
```

7. Lift the finger, completing the swipe gesture.

```
driver.perform(singletonList(sequence));
```

8. Execute the complete gesture sequence using the perform() method.

Other Ways to Perform a Gesture

While the W3C Actions API offers the most powerful and standardized way to perform gestures, Appium also supports several alternative methods, each suited to different use cases or preferences. One of the older, now deprecated, methods is the TouchAction and MultiTouchAction classes provided by the Appium client libraries. These were higher-level abstractions for performing gestures such as tap, long press, swipe, and pinch. However, due to their noncompliance with the W3C standard and limited

CHAPTER 8   ALL YOU NEED TO KNOW ON GESTURES

flexibility, they have been phased out in favor of the more robust Actions API. In addition to this, Appium exposes mobile-specific gesture commands through the mobile: script execution interface. These commands allow users to perform gestures like mobile: swipe, mobile: scroll, or mobile: dragGesture directly via script, often with simpler syntax.

For example, on Android using the UIAutomator2 driver, you can simulate a swipe by executing a command like driver.executeScript("mobile: swipeGesture", args), where args is a map containing direction or coordinates.

Similarly, on iOS using XCUITest, gestures like pinch, scroll, and tap can be executed using respective mobile: commands tailored to iOS behaviors. Finally, there's the Appium Gestures Plugin (https://github.com/AppiumTestDistribution/appium-gestures-plugin), a powerful addition to Appium's plugin ecosystem. This plugin provides high-level, ready-to-use commands for common gestures and abstracts away the complexity of writing low-level action sequences. Once installed and enabled, it offers an easier and faster way to perform gestures with minimal configuration, which is particularly useful for teams that want to simplify their test scripts while retaining gesture accuracy.

Code example for iOS and Android using mobile:

iOS example

```
Map<String, Object> args = new HashMap<>();
args.put("duration", 1.5);
args.put("fromX", 100);
args.put("fromY", 100);
args.put("toX", 300);
args.put("toY", 600);
driver.executeScript("mobile: dragFromToForDuration", args);
```

Android example

```
driver.executeScript("mobile: dragGesture", ImmutableMap.of(
    "elementId", element.getId(),
    "endX", 100,
    "endY", 100
));
```

If we have action code in the client source that is good and meets the above contract, but its execution does not produce the expected results, the following debugging methods will help.

- Make sure the gesture has valid coordinates and respects the pauses between pointer state changes. For example, it is always required to provide a valid element or absolute coordinates to any gesture at the start. iOS only recognizes a long touch/click if the pointer is held down for more than 500 ms. For shorter actions, a single click is recorded instead.

- If your tests run on Simulator, you can enable pointer tracing by enabling the appium:simulatorTracePointer capability or by disabling Visual Indicators items in the Simulator settings. After running your automation code with this feature enabled, you will be able to see the precise pointer trace path and the velocity of the gesture. Compare the trace to how the same gesture is normally performed manually, and make the necessary changes to your code.

- Do not mix WebView and native elements in action arguments. It simply won't work. Native actions could only consume native elements. To perform a native action on a web element, simply translate its coordinates into the native context and pass them as native action arguments.

Summary

This chapter analyzes the WebDriver W3C Actions API, which provides the standardized foundation for simulating complex user interactions in Appium, particularly for mobile automation. It introduces the concept of input sources, such as virtual fingers for touchscreens, and describes how actions like pointerDown, pointerMove, and pointerUp are grouped into time-based sequences called ticks. This architecture allows testers to simulate real-world gestures like swipes, drags, pinches, and multitouch interactions with precision and synchronization. A detailed example demonstrates how to implement a horizontal swipe gesture using the Java client, breaking down each step from locating the element to performing the complete action sequence. The chapter

CHAPTER 8   ALL YOU NEED TO KNOW ON GESTURES

also discusses alternative methods for gesture execution, including the deprecated TouchAction and MultiTouchAction classes, the mobile: script interface for platform-specific gesture commands, and the Appium Gestures Plugin, which offers high-level gesture abstractions. Together, these approaches provide testers and developers with both low-level control and simplified options for automating realistic mobile interactions across Android and iOS platforms.

CHAPTER 9

Build Appium Plugin

What We Will Learn

In this chapter, you will learn how to build an Appium plugin to extend and customize Appium's functionality. You will explore the purpose of plugins, how they integrate with Appium's command execution process, and how to develop a plugin from scratch. This chapter will guide you through creating a **custom logging plugin** that enhances test reporting by capturing detailed execution logs. You will also learn how to install, test, and use your plugin in an Appium session, along with best practices for maintaining and optimizing your plugin.

What the Plugin Can Do?

Appium plugins extend the core functionality of the Appium server by intercepting and modifying commands before they are executed. They act as middleware, sitting between the client request and the actual execution by the Appium driver. This allows developers to customize and enhance Appium's behavior without altering its core code.

When a test automation script sends a request, such as finding an element, click or any command that Appium supports the request first reaches the Appium server. Normally, the server processes the request and forwards it to the appropriate driver (e.g., XCUITest for iOS or UIAutomator2 for Android). Appium plugins are not limited to observing or modifying commands. They can also extend existing drivers by adding entirely new commands. Appium supports both the traditional HTTP interface and the newer WebSocket-based BiDi (bidirectional) protocol, allowing plugins to interact with either.

When a plugin is enabled, it can hook into the command lifecycle at various stages. This gives it the ability to observe, modify, or extend a command behavior before it reaches the driver, enabling advanced customization and control.

Before creating your plugin, it's important to have a clear understanding of its purpose and feasibility within the constraints of the Appium platform. This guide will help you explore what's possible. Appium's plugin system is highly flexible, with no artificial limitations imposed on its capabilities. However, due to their powerful nature, plugins are opt-in and must be explicitly enabled when starting the Appium server.

Create Project Skeleton

Step 1: Initialize the Project

Run the following command to create a new Node.js project:

```
mkdir appium-logging-plugin && cd appium-logging-plugin
npm init -y
```

This creates a `package.json` file with default values.

Step 2: Update package.json

Modify package.json to include Appium as a peer dependency and add the Appium extension metadata:

```
{
  "name": "appium-logging-plugin",
  "version": "1.0.0",
  "description": "A sample Appium plugin",
  "main": "index.js",
  "scripts": {
    "test": "echo \"No tests yet\" && exit 0"
  },
  "author": "Your Name",
  "license": "MIT",
  "peerDependencies": {
    "appium": "^2.x.x"
  },
```

```
  "appium": {
    "pluginName": "logging",
    "mainClass": "LoggingPlugin"
  }
}
```

Key Points

- **peerDependencies**: Ensures compatibility with Appium 2.x. Always use the latest version of Appium 2.x so that all the plugin building blocks are available for authors and no compatibility issues are encountered.

- **appium field**
  - **pluginName**: A short name for the plugin (logging).
  - **mainClass**: The name of the class that extends BasePlugin.

Step 3: Install Dependencies

Install Appium's base plugin package:

```
npm install --save @appium/base-plugin
```

This package provides the necessary classes and methods to build the plugin.

Step 4: Create the Plugin Class

Now, let's create the main plugin file **index.js** with a basic structure:

```
import {BasePlugin} from 'appium/plugin';
export class LoggingPlugin extends BasePlugin {
}
```

Now that we have set up the basic structure of our Appium plugin, let's take a deeper dive into what a plugin can do. We'll explore the different functionalities a plugin can enhance, the methods it can override, and how to discover these methods within Appium's architecture.

Intercept and Handle Specific Appium Commands

One of the primary capabilities of Appium plugins is modifying or completely replacing the execution of commands that would normally be handled by the active driver. This allows developers to intercept commands, customize their behavior, or introduce entirely new functionalities without altering Appium's core code.

To override default command handling, a plugin must implement asynchronous methods whose names exactly match the Appium commands they intend to modify. This approach is similar to how Appium drivers themselves define and handle commands.

How to Identify Supported Command Names?

If you're unsure which command names are available for customization, you can refer to the routes.js (`https://github.com/appium/appium/blob/master/packages/base-driver/lib/protocol/routes.js`) file in the Appium base driver. This file defines all the command routes that Appium supports. Additionally, plugins can introduce new commands beyond those defined in the base driver, as explained in the next section.

Understanding Command Method Parameters

When an Appium plugin overrides a command, the method receives several key arguments that provide control over how the command is processed:

1. **next (Function)**
   - This is an asynchronous function representing the default command execution flow.
   - If your plugin modifies a command but still wants to allow Appium's original handling to occur, you must call `await next()` at some point in your logic.
   - If `next()` is **not** called, the default behavior (including any other plugins registered after yours) will not execute.
   - This gives plugins full control over whether a command is executed, modified, or blocked entirely.

Example

```
async findElement(next, driver, strategy, selector) {
  console.log(`Intercepted findElement: ${strategy}, ${selector}`);
  return await next(); // Allow normal execution after logging
}
```

2. **driver (Object)**

    - Represents the active driver instance managing the current session.
    - Gives access to various driver properties and methods, such as retrieving session details, checking capabilities, or calling other Appium driver methods.
    - This is useful for modifying behavior based on device type, platform version, or automation settings.

Example

```
async setValue(next, driver, elementId, value) {
  if (driver.caps.platformName === 'iOS') {
    console.log('Applying iOS-specific input handling');
  }
  return await next();
}
```

3. **...args (Array)**

    - A spread array containing all user-provided arguments for the command.
    - This allows the plugin to inspect, modify, or validate command inputs before execution.

Example

```
async click(next, driver, elementId) {
  console.log(`Element clicked: ${elementId}`);
  return await next();
}
```

Putting It All Together

By leveraging these parameters, Appium plugins can intercept and log commands for debugging purposes, providing greater visibility into command execution. They can also modify inputs before they reach the driver, ensuring that the correct data is processed. Additionally, plugins allow developers to implement custom behaviors for specific commands, tailoring automation workflows to unique requirements. In cases where certain commands need to be restricted, plugins can prevent their execution, enhancing control over test scenarios. Beyond modifying existing commands, plugins can also introduce entirely new functionalities, extending Appium's capabilities to meet specialized automation needs.

Intercepting and Handling All Appium Commands

In some cases, you might want to monitor or modify all Appium commands rather than just specific ones. This can be useful for logging, debugging, or any form of global command processing. To achieve this, you can implement the async handle method in your plugin class.

Whenever a command is executed that is **not explicitly handled** by one of your named methods, it will automatically be processed by the handle method instead. This provides a centralized way to inspect and act upon all incoming commands.

Parameters of the handle Method

The method receives the following arguments, with the same semantics as in named command overrides:

- **next**: An asynchronous function representing the default command execution flow. Calling await next() allows the original command to proceed as usual.

- **driver**: The active driver instance managing the current session.

- **cmdName**: A string representing the name of the command being executed.

- **...args**: A spread array containing any arguments passed to the command by the user.

Example: Logging Command Execution Time

Let's say we want to track execution time for all Appium commands in our plugin. We can achieve this by implementing the handle method as follows:

```
async handle(next, driver, cmdName, ...args) {
  const start = process.hrtime(); // Record the start time
  try {
    return await next(); // Execute the command
  } finally {
    const elapsedMs = Date.now() - start; // Calculate execution time
    this.log(`Command '${cmdName}' took ${elapsedMs} ms`); // Log the duration
  }
}
```

How this works:

1. The start timestamp is recorded before executing the command.

2. The next() function is called to allow the command to run as expected.

3. After execution, the time taken to process the command is calculated.

4. The command name and its execution time are logged.

5. Finally, the result of the command is returned to the caller.

This approach is particularly useful for performance monitoring, debugging, or auditing Appium sessions. By implementing the handle function, you gain visibility into every command executed and can apply global modifications or enhancements as needed.

Now that we have seen how to intercept all Appium commands and also selective ones, there are certain times you need to throw certain errors and make sure the errors are W3C standard with respective HTTP status and error code.

CHAPTER 9   BUILD APPIUM PLUGIN

For example:

The plugin is handling the findElement command completely in this case; when the plugin needs to throw 404 element not found exception, then we can use the errors from the appium/driver.

Importing appium/driver in the plugin allows access to the same base driver as the Appium server setup and the minimum version specified in the peerDependencies. This is the correct approach because we expect foundation module versions to always match the umbrella driver and all extensions.

If we add @appium/base-driver, it means we want to include the base driver modules, which are a direct dependency of this extension and may differ from the umbrella driver's version. This approach is not recommended for foundation components because it may cause problems in the future when the user attempts to install the plugin.

```
import {errors} from 'appium/driver';
async findElement(next, driver, strategy, selector) {
console.log(`Intercepted findElement: ${strategy}, ${selector}`);
throw new errors.NoSuchElementError();
}
```

All the error methods can be found here, and this should not be imported directly in the code: https://github.com/appium/appium/blob/master/packages/base-driver/lib/protocol/errors.js.

Method name	Error code	HTTP status	Description
ElementClickInterceptedError	element click intercepted	400	The element click command could not be completed because the element receiving the events is obscuring the element that was requested.
ElementNotSelectableError	element not selectable	400	An attempt was made to select an element that cannot be selected.

(*continued*)

142

Method name	Error code	HTTP status	Description
ElementNotInteractableError	element not interactable	400	A command could not be completed because the element is not pointer or keyboard interactable.
InsecureCertificateError	insecure certificate	400	Caused the user agent to hit a certificate warning, which is usually the result of an expired or invalid TLS certificate.
InvalidArgumentError	invalid argument	400	The arguments passed to a command are either invalid or malformed.
InvalidCookieDomainError	invalid cookie domain	400	An illegal attempt was made to set a cookie under a different domain than the current page.
InvalidCoordinatesError	invalid coordinates	400	The coordinates provided to an interactions operation are invalid.
InvalidElementStateError	invalid element state	400	A command could not be completed because the element is in an invalid state, e.g., attempting to click an element that is no longer attached to the document.
InvalidSelectorError	invalid selector	400	Argument was an invalid selector.
InvalidSessionIdError	invalid session id	404	Occurs if the given session ID is not in the list of active sessions, meaning the session either does not exist or that it's not active.
JavaScriptError	javascript error	500	An error occurred while executing JavaScript supplied by the user.

(continued)

Method name	Error code	HTTP status	Description
`MoveTargetOutOfBoundsError`	move target out of bounds	500	The target for mouse interaction is not in the browser's viewport and cannot be brought into that viewport.
`NoSuchAlertError`	no such alert	400	An attempt was made to operate on a modal dialog when one was not open.
`NoSuchCookieError`	no such cookie	404	No cookie matching the given path name was found among the associated cookies of the current browsing context's active document.
`NoSuchElementError`	no such element	404	An element could not be located on the page using the given search parameters.
`NoSuchFrameError`	no such frame	400	A command to switch to a frame could not be satisfied because the frame could not be found.
`NoSuchWindowError`	no such window	400	A command to switch to a window could not be satisfied because the window could not be found.
`ScriptTimeoutError`	script timeout	408	A script did not complete before its timeout expired.
`SessionNotCreatedError`	session not created	500	A new session could not be created.
`StaleElementReferenceError`	stale element reference	400	A command failed because the referenced element is no longer attached to the DOM.

(continued)

Method name	Error code	HTTP status	Description
`TimeoutError`	timeout	408	An operation did not complete before its timeout expired.
`UnableToSetCookieError`	unable to set cookie	500	A command to set a cookie's value could not be satisfied.
`UnableToCaptureScreenError`	unable to capture screen	500	A screen capture was made impossible.
`UnexpectedAlertOpenError`	unexpected alert open	500	A modal dialog was open, blocking this operation.
`UnknownCommandError`	unknown command	404	A command could not be executed because the remote end is not aware of it.
`UnknownError`	unknown error	500	An unknown error occurred in the remote end while processing the command.
`UnknownMethodError`	unknown method	405	The requested command matched a known URL but did not match a method for that URL.
`UnsupportedOperationError`	unsupported operation	500	Indicates that a command that should have executed properly cannot be supported for some reason.

These are all the error codes that the appium/driver holds which helps the plugin to implement them.

Adding CLI Arguments to the Appium Plugin

Just like the Appium server accepts CLI arguments, plugins can also expose their own CLI options to allow users to configure their behavior dynamically. To achieve this, you need to define a **schema** in your package.json. This schema ensures that the plugin correctly parses and validates the provided CLI arguments.

Here's an example of how to define a schema for a plugin:

```
"schema": {
  "$schema": "http://json-schema.org/draft-07/schema",
  "additionalProperties": false,
  "description": "Appium configuration schema for the Device Farm plugin.",
  "properties": {
    "platform": {
      "type": "string"
    },
    "loggingEnabled": {
      "type": "boolean",
      "default": true
    }
  }
}
```

Breakdown of the schema:

- **$schema**: Specifies the JSON Schema version

- **additionalProperties**: Ensures that only the defined properties are allowed

- **description**: Describes the purpose of this configuration schema

- **properties**

- **platform**: A string value that can specify the platform the plugin should work with

- **loggingEnabled**: A Boolean flag (default: true) to enable or disable logging

Once added, these CLI arguments can be used when starting the plugin by – plugin-logging-logging-enabled, allowing users to control plugin behavior without modifying code.

CHAPTER 9   BUILD APPIUM PLUGIN

Overloading Execute Script

The **Execute Method** strategy is a common design pattern used in official Appium drivers and third-party extensions to execute custom commands. This pattern is based on WebDriver's executeScript mechanism, which is typically used in browser automation but has been extended for mobile automation in Appium.

How the Execute Script Command Works in WebDriver

In the context of WebDriver-based browser automation, the executeScript command allows running JavaScript code inside the browser. Let's take an example:
   javascript code:

```
await driver.executeScript('return arguments[0] + arguments[1]', [3, 4]);
```

Here's what happens:

1. The test script defines a JavaScript function body (return arguments[0] + arguments[1]).

2. The client library serializes this function and sends it over an HTTP request to the WebDriver server.

3. The WebDriver server executes the JavaScript function in the browser's context.

4. The return value of the function (7 in this case) is sent back to the client.

Each client library (WebdriverIO, Java, Python, Ruby, C#) has its own syntax for calling executeScript, but the function itself remains a **string**, ensuring consistency across different programming languages.

How the Execute Method Works in Appium

Unlike Selenium/WebDriver, Appium is usually not automating a web browser, so executeScript is **not always applicable**. However, Appium extends the executeScript concept to execute arbitrary driver-specific commands using a strategy called the **Execute Method**.

Instead of passing JavaScript code, Appium allows the user to provide a **named string** corresponding to a known driver-specific command, along with parameters.

Example: Terminating an iOS app using Execute Method

The XCUITest driver provides a way to terminate an iOS application using mobile: terminateApp. Instead of running JavaScript, this command instructs the driver to terminate a specified app by its bundleId.

Here's how the terminateApp Execute Method is used:

WebdriverIO (JavaScript)

```
await driver.executeScript('mobile: terminateApp', { bundleId: 'com.example.myapp' });
```

Java

```
driver.executeScript("mobile: terminateApp", ImmutableMap.of("bundleId", "com.example.myapp"));
```

Python

```
driver.execute_script("mobile: terminateApp", {"bundleId": "com.example.myapp"})
```

C#

```
driver.ExecuteScript("mobile: terminateApp", new Dictionary<string, object> { { "bundleId", "com.example.myapp" } });
```

Now let's see how we can implement a new method map in plugin.

Here's an example of how an Appium plugin can introduce a custom command called customLog: logMessage to enhance logging.

1. Defining executeMethodMap

```
static executeMethodMap = {
  'customLog: logMessage': {
    command: 'logCustomMessage',
    params: { required: ['message', 'level'] },
  },
};
```

CHAPTER 9   BUILD APPIUM PLUGIN

- This object defines a new command called customLog: logMessage.
- The command field maps to the method name (logCustomMessage) that will handle this command.
- The params object specifies that the command requires two parameters:
  - message: The log message to be recorded.
  - level: The severity level (e.g., info, warn, error).

2. Implementing the command logic

```
async logCustomMessage(next, driver, message, level) {
  const timestamp = new Date().toISOString();
  console.log(`[${timestamp}] [${level.toUpperCase()}] ${message}`);
  return `Logged: ${message} at ${level} level`;
}
```

- This function is the implementation of logCustomMessage.
- It receives four parameters:
  - next: A reference to the next function in the command execution chain
  - driver: The Appium driver instance
  - message: The log message
  - level: The log severity level
- The function records the log entry with a timestamp and returns a confirmation string.
- This could be further enhanced by storing logs in a file or sending them to an external logging service.

3. Overriding the Execute Method

```
async execute(next, driver, script, args) {
  return await this.executeMethod(next, driver, script, args);
}
```

- This method ensures that when an executeScript call is made, our custom Execute Method is properly processed.
- It receives four parameters:
  - next: The next function in the execution chain
  - driver: The Appium driver instance
  - script: The name of the command being executed
  - args: Any arguments passed to the command
- Instead of manually handling execution logic, this method simply delegates the execution to executeMethod, which is a helper function provided by Appium's BasePlugin class.

How Plugin Overrides Work

When a test script calls driver.executeScript('customLog: logMessage', { message: 'Test started', level: 'info' }), Appium's execution flow works as follows:

1. Appium receives the executeScript command.
2. It checks if any **plugin** has overridden this command.
3. Since our plugin defines customLog: logMessage, it **intercepts the command** and executes logCustomMessage.
4. If the command name matches an existing method in the **driver itself**, Appium gives priority to the plugin.
5. If the plugin wishes, it can invoke the original driver's behavior by calling next().If multiple pluings are enabled, then each plugin would intercept the command in the same order they are enabled in the server arguments.

Add Custom Plugin Scripts

Sometimes we might want the plugin to be able to run scripts outside the context of a session (e.g., to run a script that prebuilds aspects to the plugin). To support this, we can add a map of script names and JS files to the scripts field within your Appium extension metadata. So let's say we created a script in our project that lives in a scripts directory, named plugin-prebuild.js. Then you could add a scripts field like this:

```
{
    "scripts": {
        "prebuild": "./scripts/plugin-prebuild.js"
    }
}
```

We can start plugin as "**appium plugin run logging prebuild**", and your script will execute.

Summary

This chapter explored the fundamentals of **building an Appium plugin**, providing insights into how plugins extend Appium's functionality by intercepting and modifying commands.

We started with an overview of **how Appium plugins work**, explaining how they integrate with the Appium server to enhance automation capabilities. Plugins can hook into the command execution process, modify behavior, log additional information, or introduce entirely new commands. Here is a sample project read and try https://github.com/appium/appium/tree/master/packages/fake-plugin.

Next, we introduced the **Execute Method strategy**, a pattern widely used in Appium drivers and plugins. We examined how the executeScript command works across different WebDriver client libraries and discussed its adaptation in Appium for executing mobile-specific commands.

We then discussed **overriding Execute Method**, demonstrating how plugins can define and implement custom commands. Using a **custom logging plugin** as an example, we showed how to

- **Define an Execute Method map** to register new commands.
- **Implement command logic** to process incoming requests (e.g., logging messages with severity levels).
- **Override the execute function** to ensure seamless command handling while maintaining Appium's core functionality.

CHAPTER 9   BUILD APPIUM PLUGIN

Finally, we discussed **how plugin overrides work**, explaining that if a plugin defines an Execute Method with the same name as an existing Appium driver method, the plugin's version takes precedence. However, developers have the flexibility to invoke the original driver behavior when needed.

By the end of this chapter, you should have a clear understanding of how to create, register, and extend Appium plugins to introduce custom functionalities. This knowledge empowers you to tailor Appium automation to your specific needs, whether it's enhancing logging, modifying command behavior, or integrating with external systems.

CHAPTER 10

Optimizing and Troubleshooting Appium Tests

What You Will Learn

This chapter covers essential strategies for improving the performance, reliability, and efficiency of Appium tests. You will gain insights into optimizing test execution, handling synchronization challenges, reducing test execution time, and troubleshooting common issues. By applying these best practices, you can ensure a stable and efficient mobile automation framework.

Performance Optimization for iOS Real Device Tests

Running tests on real iOS devices can be time-consuming due to the need to build and deploy WebDriverAgent (WDA) for each session. This process involves compiling WDA, signing it with the appropriate developer profile, installing it on the device, and launching it before any test execution can begin. Each of these steps causes delays, particularly when testing frequently. So the best option is to handle the WebDriverAgent ourselves.

Prebuild WebDriverAgent

Instead of allowing Appium to rebuild WDA every time a session starts, manually build and install WDA on the device beforehand. This can be done using Xcode, ensuring that assigned, working WDA instances are available on the device at all times. This significantly reduces session startup time and prevents unnecessary compilation overhead.

Most importantly, WDA must be rebuilt for each new version of driver update; otherwise, an older WDA version is cached on the device and may be incompatible with the actual XCUITest driver.

Setting Up WebDriverAgent

WebDriverAgent (WDA) is automatically downloaded as part of the XCUITest driver package which is a direct dependency. When you install the driver using `appium driver install xcuitest`, the WebDriverAgent module is placed in $APPIUM_HOME/node_modules/appium-xcuitest-driver/node_modules/appium-webdriveragent. By default, APPIUM_HOME is located at ~/.appium.

For real devices, additional configuration is required due to Apple's security policies. You must configure code signing correctly. Follow the **Real Device Configuration** guide to complete the code signing setup.

To ensure WDA is properly configured:

1. Open $APPIUM_HOME/node_modules/appium-xcuitest-driver/node_modules/appium-webdriveragent/WebDriverAgent.xcodeproj in Xcode.

2. Select the **WebDriverAgentRunner** project.

3. Choose your real device or simulator as the build target.

4. From Xcode's main menu, navigate to **Product ➤ Test** (refer to Figure 3-2).

5. Xcode should successfully build the project and install it on the real device or simulator. You should see the **WebDriverAgentRunner** application icon on the device's home screen.

This way the WDA is installed on the device, but when running on CI environments, it's best to build the WDA as IPA so that we can install the WDA as any other application on the device. We have already discussed this in Chapter 3 under section "Steps to Create a WebDriverAgent IPA." Let's understand next on how to install WDA on device/simulator and also make sure it's running before the tests is started.

WebDriverAgent Initialization and Connectivity

WebDriverAgent functions as a REST server that forwards external API requests to native XCTest calls in your application under test. The server runs at `localhost` for simulators and the real device's IP address when testing on physical hardware.

To unify WDA's network address for both simulators and real devices, Appium uses `appium-ios-device` to route network requests via USB, ensuring seamless communication. If the test project is in the node.js/typescript tech stack, then we can also use the appium-ios-device module and reuse things. But what if the test automation framework is writing in Java or any other client bindings, then we need to handle this on our own. So to do this, there are multiple open source libraries which can help us to connect with real devices.

You can also manage WDA connections manually using alternative tools:

- **iproxy**: Installed via `npm install -g iproxy`, enabling port forwarding for remote connections

- **go-ios**: A command-line tool for managing iOS devices, including WDA

- **tidevice**: A Python-based tool for managing and interacting with iOS devices

So let's see code examples for both Node.js and Java.

Making WDA Readiness in Node.js

Since we have the WDA.ipa prepared, let's use the open source library to install the application on a real device. Let's consider go-ios as this library is well maintained by the community and is widely used.

CHAPTER 10   OPTIMIZING AND TROUBLESHOOTING APPIUM TESTS

1. Run the command (Refer to Figure 10-1)

Figure 10-1. *go-ios installation*

2. Next, let's install the WDA on a real device. If no –udid is given, then it will install on the first available device. Refer to Figure 10-2.

Figure 10-2. *Install WDA*

3. Once the WDA is installed on the device, we need to start the WDA on a real device; before that, we need to proxy the system IP to the device so that once WDA as a server is running inside the device, we will be able to make a HTTP request to that server. Refer to Figure 10-3.

Figure 10-3. *Port forward*

CHAPTER 10   OPTIMIZING AND TROUBLESHOOTING APPIUM TESTS

4. Now as the port forward is executed successfully, we need to start the WDA application using the go-ios module.

Below is the code example in Node.js to install and launch WDA.

```
export async function installIPA(path: any, udid: string): Promise<void> {
    const command = `${goIOS} install --udid=${udid} --path=${path}`;
    const { stdout, stderr } = await asyncExec(command);
    console.log(`stdout: ${stdout}`);
    console.error(`stderr: ${stderr}`);
try {
    const launchWDA = `${goIOS} runwda --udid=${udid} --bundleid=${appBundleId}    --testrunnerbundleid=${appBundleId} --xctest config=WebDriverAgentRunner.xctest --env  USE_PORT=${device.wdaLocalPort} --env MJPEG_SERVER_PORT=${device.mjpegServerPort}`;
console.log(launchWDA);
exec(launchWDA, (error, stdout, stderr) => {
if (error) {
    console.error(`exec error: ${error}`);
return;
}
console.log(`stdout: ${stdout}`);
console.error(`stderr: ${stderr}`);
});
} catch (error) {
console.error(`Error executing command: ${error}`);
}
}
```

Now add the appium capability webDriverAgentUrl=http://systemIP:8100: specifies a direct connection to a prelaunched WDA instance, further reducing session initialization time.

Once the webDriverAgentUrl capability is specified, Appium will not take steps of WDA process; it will just try to connect to the AgentUrl.

This way we can completely solve the test startup time for iOS real devices.

Handling OTP Field Input Using W3C Actions

A common challenge in mobile test automation is entering OTP (one-time password) values into input fields. Traditional sendKeys methods may not always work reliably, particularly when dealing with secure input fields. To address this issue, Appium provides W3C Actions, which allow for simulating key presses more effectively.

Using W3C Actions for OTP Input

Instead of relying on sendKeys, W3C Actions can be used to enter OTP digits one by one, mimicking real user input. The following implementation demonstrates how to achieve this:

```
await driver.performActions([setValue(source?.value)]);
export function setValue(result) {
  log.info('Setting value:', result);
  const setValueActions = result
    .split('')
    .map((char) => [
      { type: 'keyDown', value: char },
      { type: 'keyUp', value: char },
    ])
    .flat();
  const actionsData = {
    type: 'key',
    id: 'keyboard',
    actions: setValueActions,
  };
  return actionsData;
}
```

Tap on Element at Specific Location

By default, when Appium performs a click action on an element, it clicks at the center of the element. However, there are scenarios where you may need to tap on a specific position within the element rather than its center. The following section explores how to achieve precise tapping at a defined location within an element. Refer to Figure 10-4 for reference.

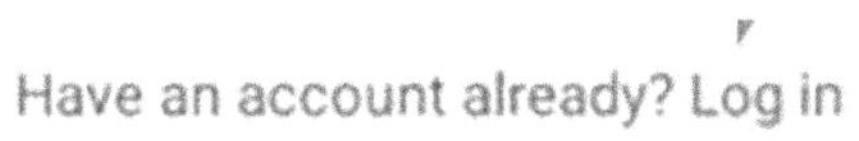

Have an account already? Log in

Figure 10-4. Partial click

In this scenario, we need to tap on the "Log in" link, which is positioned at the end of the element. Instead of using element.click(), which clicks at the center by default, we can utilize the Actions API to achieve precise tapping. First, we retrieve the element object and use getRect() to obtain the element's top-left coordinates, along with its width and height. Using these values, we can then calculate the exact x and y coordinates needed to perform the click at the desired location.

```
async function tapAtPosition(driver, point) {
    const actions = [
        {
            type: "pointer",
            id: "finger1",
            parameters: { pointerType: "touch" },
            actions: [
                { type: "pointerMove", duration: 0, x: point.x, y: point.y,
                origin: "viewport" },
                { type: "pointerDown", button: 0 },
                { type: "pause", duration: 200 },
                { type: "pointerUp", button: 0 }
            ]
        }
    ];
    await driver.performActions(actions);
}
```

```
async function tapElementPosition(element, xPercent, yPercent) {
    const rect = await element.getRect();
    const point = {
        x: rect.x + Math.floor(rect.width * xPercent),
        y: rect.y + Math.floor(rect.height * yPercent)
    };

    await tapAtPosition(driver, point);
}
Usage:
async function tapElement(element) {
    tapElementPosition(element, 0.9, 0.5)
}
```

1. **tapElement**

   - Accepts **relative percentages** (xPercent, yPercent) instead of absolute pixels
   - Calculates the exact coordinates dynamically based on the element's dimensions
   - Works consistently across different screen sizes and resolutions

2. **tapElementPosition**

   - Demonstrates how to tap at **90% from the left** and **50% from the top**, useful for elements with interactive regions

This approach makes it **scalable and adaptable** for different UI layouts!

Capturing Multiple Screenshots Efficiently in Test Execution

When running automated mobile tests, capturing screenshots is a common practice for debugging and validation. However, **taking screenshots in Appium can be slow**, with each capture taking around **200 ms**. This delay becomes a bottleneck when multiple screenshots are needed in a test suite.

Scenario

Consider a test case where you need to capture screenshots at every step of a complex user journey, such as

- **Filling out a multistep form**
- **Navigating through different screens in an app**
- **Capturing UI state changes at critical points**

If a test requires **50 screenshots**, the standard screenshot method would take **10 seconds (50 × 200 ms)**, slowing down execution. Reducing the capture time would drastically improve test efficiency.

Enabling MJPEG Server for Faster Screenshots

Appium provides an **MJPEG Server**, compresses screenshots as low-quality jpeg images, and pushes them to one or more consumer in an async thread using options provided by mjpegServerFramerate, mjpegScalingFactor, and mjpegServerScreenshotQuality. All mentioned settings are configured for optimal performance rather than quality. By setting the `mjpegServerPort` and `mjpegScreenshotUrl`, Appium reduces screenshot latency from **200 ms to just ~30 ms**.

- This allows tests that require **frequent screenshots** to run much faster.
- The performance boost significantly reduces execution time without compromising test coverage.

Managing Contexts in Appium

Modern mobile applications often integrate both native and web-based components within the same app. This hybrid approach allows developers to **embed web content** inside a native app frame, leveraging existing web technologies for specific app features. However, this introduces a **challenge for automation tools** like Appium, which are primarily designed to interact with native elements.

CHAPTER 10   OPTIMIZING AND TROUBLESHOOTING APPIUM TESTS

When a mobile app contains web-based content (such as a WebView in Android or an WKWebView in iOS), automation tools must **switch between different contexts**—one for native components and another for web content.

Actually, WebViews also provide a native view of their elements, although this view is limited in comparison to the one available through the web debugger interface, which means that the possibility to switch between contexts enriches automation possibilities. Appium provides a **Context API** that enables automation scripts to identify and interact with the appropriate mode, ensuring smooth test execution across **native, web, and hybrid apps**.

Understanding Appium Contexts

In Appium, a **context** represents the execution environment of an application. An application can have one or more contexts, and Appium allows switching between them dynamically.

Here's how different contexts work:

- **Native Context (`NATIVE_APP`)**: Represent the structure that the application exposes to the system accessibility framework, at least in these two drivers. This is the default context and allows interaction with native elements using UI automation frameworks like **XCUITest (iOS)** and **UiAutomator2 (Android)**.

- **WebView Contexts**: Enables access to the same stack that the browser engine web debugger has access to. When an app uses a WebView, Appium allows switching into a WebView context, enabling interaction using web automation commands similar to Selenium.

Context Management API in Appium

Appium extends the **W3C WebDriver specification** by introducing a set of commands to manage different contexts within an app. These commands allow automation scripts to detect available contexts, retrieve the active context, and switch between them as needed.

Command name	Method/route	Parameters	Description	Returns
Get Contexts	GET /session/:id/contexts	None	Retrieves a list of available contexts in the current session (e.g., native app, WebViews)	Array<string>
Get Current Context	GET /session/:id/context	None	Returns the name of the active context in the session	String
Set Context	POST /session/:id/context	name (string)	Switches to the specified context by name	null

How Contexts Work in Different Appium Drivers

The interpretation of contexts may vary depending on the Appium driver being used.

Example: Context Handling in XCUITest (iOS)

For iOS applications automated with the **XCUITest driver**, the available contexts typically include

1. **NATIVE_APP**: The default context for interacting with native elements.

2. **WebView Contexts**: Each WebView in the app appears as a separate context.

A call to Get Contexts in an iOS app with an active WebView might return:

["NATIVE_APP", "WEBVIEW_1"]

Switching to the WebView context allows automation scripts to interact with web elements inside the app:

driver.context("WEBVIEW_1");

When in a WebView context, Appium interacts with elements using **Selenium-like web automation techniques** rather than native UI automation.

CHAPTER 10   OPTIMIZING AND TROUBLESHOOTING APPIUM TESTS

Example: Context Handling in UiAutomator2 (Android)

For Android applications using the **UiAutomator2 driver and iOS applications using XCUITest Driver**, the process is similar. However, WebViews must be **explicitly enabled for debugging** before they can be detected by Appium.

A call to Get Contexts in an Android app with WebView content might return:

```
["NATIVE_APP", "WEBVIEW_com.example"]
```

Switching to the WebView allows automation of web-based elements inside the app:

```
driver.context("WEBVIEW_com.example");
```

Key Considerations When Managing Contexts

1. **The Default Context Is Always Native (NATIVE_APP)**

    - When launching an Appium session, the **default active context** is the native app context if the browserName capability is not explicitly mentioned.

    - Calling Get Contexts will **always** return at least one context, typically "NATIVE_APP".

2. **WebView Debugging Must Be Enabled (Android)**

    For Android apps, WebView debugging must be enabled in the app using

    ```
    WebView.setWebContentsDebuggingEnabled(true);
    ```

    - If WebViews are not debuggable, Appium **will not detect them** in the context list.

3. **Switching Contexts Affects Element Locators**

    - The **locator strategies** used in different contexts vary.

    - In NATIVE_APP, you can use XPath, accessibility IDs, and native selectors.

    - In WEBVIEW, you must use CSS selectors, XPath (for web), and JavaScript-based interactions.

How to Manage Locators in React Native App

React Native has evolved into a pillar for creating cross-platform apps effectively in the fast-paced realm of mobile app creation. But as apps get more sophisticated, the challenges of implementing robust test automation increase.

Not following React Native best practices, like incorrectly identifying elements, having overly complicated DOM structures, and unintentional clashes between accessibility and testability, leads to unreliable tests, slower performance, and incorrect results in tools like Appium.

This blog explores three React Native development pillars directly influencing your Appium test suite dependability:

- **Element Identification Hierarchy**: Separating platform-specific hazards to guarantee Appium always finds elements
- **DOM Reduction Techniques**: Optimizing render logic to eliminate "ghost nodes" to accelerate test execution
- **Strategic Use of Accessibility Features**: Balancing test automation requirements with screen reader compliance

These battle-tested techniques will enable you to create apps that are both user-friendly and automation-friendly without sacrificing either front, regardless of your struggle with inconsistent test failures or slow-moving automation pipelines.

On Android, both *testID* and *accessibilityLabel* map to different native properties, but developers often misuse them interchangeably. This leads to

- **Appium Element Detection Failures**: If *accessibilityLabel* overrides *testID*-related properties on Android.
- **Accessibility Conflicts**: Screen readers might read testing identifiers instead of user-friendly labels.
- **Fragile Selectors**: Tests break when accessibility needs change.

Platform-Specific Mappings

Property	Android native property	iOS native property
testID	View Tag (view.setTag())	accessibilityIdentifier
accessibilityLabel	contentDescription	accessibilityLabel

Key Conflicts

- **Android**
  - *testID* sets a view tag or *resource-id*.
  - *accessibilityLabel* sets *contentDescription*, which Appium can see.
  - **Risk**: Developers use *accessibilityLabel* as a *testID* workaround, polluting accessibility metadata.
- **iOS**
  - **No collision**: *testID* and *accessibilityLabel* map to separate properties.

Robust Solution

1. **Separation of Concerns**
   - *testID: Exclusively for Appium element identification*
   - *accessibilityLabel: Exclusively for screen reader announcements*

```
<Button
  testID="login-submit-btn" // For Appium
  accessibilityLabel="Submit login form" // For screen readers
  accessibilityRole="button"
/>
```

2. **Platform-Specific Appium Strategies**

   Configure Appium to use the correct property for each platform:

   - **iOS**: Locate elements by accessibilityIdentifier (maps to testID)

```
driver.findElement(AppiumBy.accessibilityId("login-submit-btn"))
```

   - **Android**: Use custom locators to target viewTag(maps totestID)

```
// Custom "test-id" locator strategy for Android - For Espresso
driver.findElement(AppiumBy.androidViewTag("login-submit-btn"));
// UIAutomator2
driver.findElement(AppiumBy.androidUIAutomator("new UIAutomator().
description('login-submit-btn')"));
```

3. **Validation Workflow**

   1. **Android**

```
adb shell uiautomator dump
adb shell cat /sdcard/window_dump.xml | grep 'login-submit-btn'
```

      Verify resource-id, content-desc, and view-tag values.

   2. **iOS**

      Use Xcode's **Accessibility Inspector** to check identifier and label.

Designing with empathy for both your users and your QA processes is more than just a matter of writing better code; it is also a matter of mastering the nuances of React Native with respect to test automation

Remember this: What's good for automation is frequently good for accessibility, and vice versa, when you restructure your React Native components. Use the checklist on this site to audit your app right now and see for yourself how small changes can lead to significant improvements in quality and performance. The finest programs, after all, are created to be tested rather than merely created. More detailed examples can be found in https://www.lambdatest.com/blog/react-native-best-practices/.

CHAPTER 11

Contribute to Appium

What You Will Learn

This chapter delves into the interior workings of Appium's codebase, offering a comprehensive understanding of its architecture, key components, and the manner in which they interact to facilitate cross-platform test automation.

Appium's Monorepo Structure

Appium 3.0 and beyond is organized as a monorepo, which means that multiple related packages are managed within a single repository. This structure facilitates better code sharing, versioning, and maintenance. The main packages include

1. **appium**: The main package that serves as the entry point and command-line interface. It also includes the implementation of the umbrella AppiumDriver class used to orchestrate all other drivers.

2. **base-driver**: Provides the foundational driver functionality.

3. **base-plugin**: Offers the core plugin infrastructure.

4. **support**: Contains utility functions used across packages.

5. **types**: TypeScript-type definitions.

6. Various driver and plugin packages.

This modular approach allows Appium to maintain a clean separation of concerns while enabling extensibility through its driver and plugin systems.

CHAPTER 11   CONTRIBUTE TO APPIUM

Core Architecture Components

Appium's architecture follows a well-defined inheritance pattern:

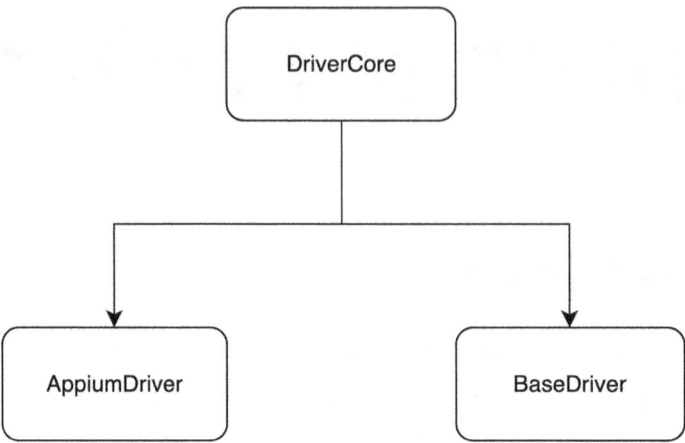

Let's examine each class in this hierarchy with code examples to understand their roles:

AppiumDriver: The top-level driver that manages other drivers, handles command routing, and coordinates plugins.

```
// From packages/appium/lib/appium.js
class AppiumDriver extends DriverCore {
  sessions;  // Map of session IDs to driver instances
  pendingDrivers;
  pluginClasses;
  sessionPlugins;
  driverConfig;

  // Command execution with plugin support
  async executeCommand(cmd, ...args) {
    // Determine if this is a session command
    const isSessionCmd = isSessionCommand(cmd);
    let sessionId = null;
    let dstSession = null;
    let driver = this;

    if (isSessionCmd) {
```

```
    sessionId = _.last(args);
    dstSession = this.sessions[sessionId];
    protocol = dstSession.protocol;
    if (!isUmbrellaCmd) {
      driver = dstSession;
    }
  }

  // Get plugins that handle this command
  const plugins = this.pluginsToHandleCmd(cmd, sessionId);

  // Define default behavior
  const defaultBehavior = async () => {
    if (isGetStatus) {
      return await this.getStatus();
    }
    if (isUmbrellaCmd) {
      return await BaseDriver.prototype.executeCommand.call(this, cmd,
        ...args);
    }
    return await dstSession.executeCommand(cmd, ...args);
  };

  // Wrap command with plugins
  const wrappedCmd = this.wrapCommandWithPlugins({
    driver, cmd, args, plugins, cmdHandledBy, next: defaultBehavior
  });

  // Execute the wrapped command
  return await this.executeWrappedCommand({wrappedCmd, protocol});
}

// Session creation with driver selection
async createSession(jsonwpCaps, reqCaps, w3cCapabilities) {
  // Find matching driver based on capabilities
  const {driver: InnerDriver, version: driverVersion} =
    await this.driverConfig.findMatchingDriver(desiredCaps);
```

```
  // Create driver instance
  const driverInstance = new InnerDriver(this.args, true);

  // Create session on the driver
  const [innerSessionId, dCaps] = await driverInstance.createSession(
    processedJsonwpCapabilities,
    reqCaps,
    processedW3CCapabilities
  );

  // Store session
  this.sessions[innerSessionId] = driverInstance;

  return [innerSessionId, dCaps];
  }
}
```

BaseDriver: Builds on DriverCore to implement WebDriver protocol handling, capabilities processing, and command execution.

```
// From packages/base-driver/lib/basedriver/driver.ts
export class BaseDriver<
    const C extends Constraints,
    CArgs extends StringRecord = StringRecord,
    Settings extends StringRecord = StringRecord,
    CreateResult = DefaultCreateSessionResult<C>,
    DeleteResult = DefaultDeleteSessionResult,
    SessionData extends StringRecord = StringRecord,
  >
  extends DriverCore<C, Settings>
  implements Driver<C, CArgs, Settings, CreateResult, DeleteResult, SessionData>
{
  cliArgs: CArgs & ServerArgs;
  caps: DriverCaps<C>;
  originalCaps: W3CDriverCaps<C>;
  desiredCapConstraints: C;
```

```
// Command execution with timeout handling
async executeCommand<T = unknown>(cmd: string, ...args: any[]):
Promise<T> {
  // Clear any existing command timeout
  await this.clearNewCommandTimeout();

  // Execute the command
  const runCommandPromise = async () => {
    return await this[cmd](...args);
  };

  // Use command queue if enabled
  const res = this.isCommandsQueueEnabled
    ? await this.commandsQueueGuard.acquire(BaseDriver.name,
    runCommandPromise)
    : await runCommandPromise();

  // Start a new command timeout
  if (this.isCommandsQueueEnabled && cmd !== DELETE_SESSION_COMMAND) {
    await this.startNewCommandTimeout();
  }

  return res;
}

// Session creation with capabilities processing
async createSession(
  w3cCapabilities1: W3CDriverCaps<C>,
  w3cCapabilities2?: W3CDriverCaps<C>,
  w3cCapabilities?: W3CDriverCaps<C>,
  driverData?: DriverData[],
): Promise<CreateResult> {
  // Process capabilities
  const originalCaps = _.cloneDeep(
    [w3cCapabilities, w3cCapabilities1, w3cCapabilities2].find(isW3cCaps)
  );

  // Validate capabilities
```

CHAPTER 11   CONTRIBUTE TO APPIUM

```
    let caps: DriverCaps<C> = processCapabilities(
      originalCaps,
      this._desiredCapConstraints,
      this.shouldValidateCaps
    );

    // Create session
    this.sessionId = util.uuidV4();
    this.sessionCreationTimestampMs = Date.now();
    this.caps = caps;

    return [this.sessionId, caps] as CreateResult;
  }
}
```

DriverCore: Extends ExtensionCore and adds core driver functionality like session management, command queuing, and feature toggling.

```
// From packages/base-driver/lib/basedriver/core.ts
export class DriverCore<const C extends Constraints, Settings extends
StringRecord = StringRecord>
  extends ExtensionCore implements Core<C, Settings>
{
  sessionId: string | null;
  sessionCreationTimestampMs: number;
  opts: DriverOpts<C>;
  initialOpts: InitialOpts;
  basePath: string;
  relaxedSecurityEnabled: boolean;
  allowInsecure: string[];
  denyInsecure: string[];
  newCommandTimeoutMs: number;
  implicitWaitMs: number;
  commandsQueueGuard: AsyncLock;

  // Feature management
  isFeatureEnabled(name: string): boolean {
    // Check if a feature is enabled based on security settings
```

```
    const currentAutomationName = _.toLower(this.opts.automationName);

    // If explicitly denied, return false
    if (!_.isEmpty(this.denyInsecure) &&
        parseFullNames(this.denyInsecure).some(matches)) {
      return false;
    }

    // If explicitly allowed, return true
    if (!_.isEmpty(this.allowInsecure) &&
        parseFullNames(this.allowInsecure).some(matches)) {
      return true;
    }

    // If relaxed security is enabled, return true
    if (this.relaxedSecurityEnabled) {
      return true;
    }

    return false;
  }

  // Command queue management
  get isCommandsQueueEnabled(): boolean {
    return true;
  }
}
```

ExtensionCore: The base class for all extensions (drivers and plugins), providing common functionality like logging and BiDi (bidirectional) command handling.

```
// From packages/base-driver/lib/basedriver/extension-core.ts
export class ExtensionCore {
  bidiEventSubs: Record<string, string[]>;
  bidiCommands: BidiModuleMap = BIDI_COMMANDS as BidiModuleMap;
  _logPrefix?: string;
  protected _log: AppiumLogger;
  readonly eventEmitter: NodeJS.EventEmitter;
```

CHAPTER 11   CONTRIBUTE TO APPIUM

```
  constructor(logPrefix?: string) {
    this._logPrefix = logPrefix;
    this.bidiEventSubs = {};
    this.eventEmitter = new EventEmitter();
  }

  // Handles BiDi (Bidirectional) commands
  async executeBidiCommand(bidiCmd: string, bidiParams: StringRecord,
  next?: () => Promise<any>, driver?: ExtensionCore) {
    const [moduleName, methodName] = bidiCmd.split('.');
    this.ensureBidiCommandExists(moduleName, methodName);
    const {command, params} = this.bidiCommands[moduleName][methodName];

    // Execute the command
    const response = (next && driver)
      ? await this[command](next, driver, ...args)
      : await this[command](...args);

    return response;
  }
}
```

This inheritance structure allows for code reuse while enabling specialization at each level. Each class in the hierarchy adds specific functionality:

- **ExtensionCore** provides the foundation for all extensions with logging and BiDi support.
- **DriverCore** adds session management and security features.
- **BaseDriver** implements the WebDriver protocol and command execution.
- **AppiumDriver** coordinates multiple drivers and plugins to handle client requests.

This modular design makes Appium highly extensible and maintainable, allowing for new drivers and plugins to be added without modifying the core code.

The Command Execution Flow

When a client sends a request to Appium, it goes through several layers of processing:

1. **HTTP Server**: The request is first received by an Express.js server configured in `server.js`.

2. **Router**: The request is routed based on the endpoint and HTTP method defined in `routes.js`.

3. **Protocol Handler**: The `protocol.js` module processes the request, validates parameters, and prepares arguments for command execution.

4. **AppiumDriver**: The umbrella driver receives the command and determines how to handle it:
   - If it's a session command, it routes to the appropriate session driver.
   - If it's a server command, it handles it directly.
   - If plugins are involved, it manages the plugin chain and might inject custom handlers.

5. **Session Driver**: The platform-specific driver (e.g., XCUITest, UiAutomator2) executes the command and returns the result.

6. **Response Formatting**: The result is formatted according to the appropriate protocol (W3C WebDriver) and sent back to the client.

Let's look at a code example from `appium.js` that shows how commands are executed:

```
async executeCommand(cmd, ...args) {
  // Determine if this is a session command
  const isSessionCmd = isSessionCommand(cmd);

  // Get the session ID if this is a session command
  let sessionId = null;
  let dstSession = null;
  let protocol = null;
  let driver = this;
```

```
  if (isSessionCmd) {
    sessionId = _.last(args);
    dstSession = this.sessions[sessionId];
    if (!dstSession) {
      throw new Error(`The session with id '${sessionId}' does not exist`);
    }
    protocol = dstSession.protocol;
    if (!isUmbrellaCmd) {
      driver = dstSession;
    }
  }

  // Get plugins that handle this command
  const plugins = this.pluginsToHandleCmd(cmd, sessionId);

  // Define the default behavior
  const defaultBehavior = async () => {
    // Execute the command on the appropriate driver
    return await driver.executeCommand(cmd, ...args);
  };

  // Wrap the command with plugins
  const wrappedCmd = this.wrapCommandWithPlugins({
    driver,
    cmd,
    args,
    plugins,
    cmdHandledBy,
    next: defaultBehavior,
  });

  // Execute the wrapped command
  const res = await this.executeWrappedCommand({wrappedCmd, protocol});

  return res;
}
```

This code demonstrates how Appium handles command execution, including plugin integration and session management.

Extension System: Drivers and Plugins

One of Appium's most powerful features is its extensibility through drivers and plugins.

Drivers

Drivers are extensions that enable Appium to automate specific platforms. Each driver implements the WebDriver protocol for a particular platform (iOS, Android, Windows, etc.). The driver system is managed through several key components:

1. **DriverConfig**: Manages driver metadata, validation, and loading
2. **Manifest**: Tracks installed drivers and their configurations
3. **Extension Loading**: Dynamically loads driver code when needed

When a session is created, Appium uses the provided capabilities to select the appropriate driver:

```
async findMatchingDriver({automationName, platformName}) {
  if (!_.isString(platformName)) {
    throw new Error('You must include a platformName capability');
  }

  if (!_.isString(automationName)) {
    throw new Error('You must include an automationName capability');
  }

  try {
    const {driverName, mainClass, version} = this._getDriverBySupport(
      automationName,
      platformName
    );
    const driver = await this.requireAsync(driverName);
    return {driver, version, driverName};
  } catch (err) {
    const msg =
      `Could not find a driver for automationName ` +
      `'${automationName}' and platformName '${platformName}'. ` +
      `Have you installed a driver that supports those ` +
```

CHAPTER 11   CONTRIBUTE TO APPIUM

```
      `capabilities?`;
    throw new Error(msg);
  }
}
```

Plugins

Plugins extend Appium's functionality without modifying the core code. They can intercept and modify commands, add new commands, or provide additional features. The plugin system works through a middleware-like pattern:

```
wrapCommandWithPlugins({driver, cmd, args, next, cmdHandledBy, plugins}) {
  if (plugins.length) {
    this.log.info(`Plugins which can handle cmd '${cmd}': ${plugins.map((p)
    => p.name)}`);
  }

  // Wrap the next function with each plugin's handler
  for (const plugin of plugins) {
    cmdHandledBy[plugin.name] = false;
    next = ((_next) => async () => {
      this.log.info(`Plugin ${plugin.name} is now handling cmd '${cmd}'`);
      cmdHandledBy[plugin.name] = true;

      // Call the plugin's command handler or generic handler
      if (plugin[cmd]) {
        return await plugin[cmd](_next, driver, ...args);
      }
      return await plugin.handle(_next, driver, cmd, ...args);
    })(next);
  }

  return next;
}
```

This pattern allows plugins to be chained together, with each plugin having the option to call the next handler or short-circuit the chain.

… CHAPTER 11 CONTRIBUTE TO APPIUM

HTTP Server and Routing

Appium's HTTP server is built on Express.js and configured in `server.js`. The server setup includes middleware for logging, CORS handling, body parsing, and error handling.

Routes are defined in `routes.js` as a mapping of endpoints to command handlers:

```
export const METHOD_MAP = {
  '/status': {
    GET: {command: 'getStatus'},
  },
  '/session': {
    POST: {
      command: 'createSession',
      payloadParams: {
        validate: (jsonObj) =>
          !jsonObj.capabilities &&
          !jsonObj.desiredCapabilities &&
          'we require one of "desiredCapabilities" or "capabilities" object',
        optional: ['desiredCapabilities', 'requiredCapabilities',
          'capabilities'],
      },
    },
  },
  // ... many more routes
}
```

Each route specifies

- The HTTP method (GET, POST, etc.)
- The command to execute
- Parameter validation rules
- Optional parameter processing instructions

The `routeConfiguringFunction` in `protocol.js` uses this map to set up all the routes when the server starts.

CHAPTER 11   CONTRIBUTE TO APPIUM

Session Management

Session management is a critical part of Appium's functionality. The `AppiumDriver` class maintains a map of session IDs to driver instances:

```
class AppiumDriver extends DriverCore {
  sessions;  // Map of session IDs to driver instances

  async createSession(jsonwpCaps, reqCaps, w3cCapabilities) {
    // Process capabilities
    // Find matching driver
    // Create driver instance
    // Store in sessions map
    this.sessions[innerSessionId] = driverInstance;
    // Return session ID and capabilities
  }

  async deleteSession(sessionId) {
    // Get the session
    const dstSession = this.sessions[sessionId];
    // Delete from sessions map
    delete this.sessions[sessionId];
    // Clean up the session
    await dstSession.deleteSession(sessionId);
  }
}
```

This approach allows Appium to route commands to the appropriate driver instance based on the session ID included in the request.

Bidirectional (BiDi) Communication

Appium 3.0 introduced support for bidirectional communication through WebSockets (https://www.w3.org/TR/webdriver-bidi/), allowing for more interactive automation scenarios. The BiDi implementation is spread across several files, with core functionality in `bidi-commands.js`.

The WebSocket server is initialized in `main.js`:

```
const bidiServer = new WebSocketServer({noServer: true});
bidiServer.on('connection', appiumDriver.onBidiConnection.
bind(appiumDriver));
bidiServer.on('error', appiumDriver.onBidiServerError.bind(appiumDriver));
server.addWebSocketHandler('/bidi', bidiServer);
server.addWebSocketHandler('/bidi/:sessionId', bidiServer);
```

This enables clients to establish WebSocket connections for real-time communication with the Appium server.

Let's look at an example of a client-created session to understand the flow between drivers.

End-to-End Flow: Creating an Android Session

To better understand how Appium works, let's trace the complete flow of a session creation request from the client all the way to the device. This example will focus on Android automation using the UiAutomator2 driver, which is one of the most commonly used drivers.

Client-Side Initialization

When a client wants to create a new Appium session for Android automation, it typically starts with code like this:

```
// Java client example
UiAutomator2Options options = new UiAutomator2Options(); options.
setPlatformName("Android"); options.setAutomationName("UiAutomator2");
options.setDeviceName("Android Device");
options.setAppPackage("com.example.app"); options.setAppActivity("com.
example.app.MainActivity"); URL appiumServerURL = new URL("http://
localhost:4723/wd/hub");
AndroidDriver driver = new AndroidDriver(appiumServerURL, options);
```

This client code does the following:

1. Sets up desired capabilities specifying the platform, automation framework, and app details
2. Creates a connection to the Appium server
3. Initializes an `AndroidDriver` instance, which sends a session creation request to the server

When the `new AndroidDriver()` is called, it triggers a chain of events:

1. **HTTP Request**: The client sends a POST request to `/session` with the desired capabilities.
2. **Express Server**: The Appium server's Express.js instance receives the request.
3. **Router**: The request is routed to the `createSession` command handler.
4. **Protocol Handler**: The protocol handler validates the capabilities and prepares arguments.
5. **AppiumDriver**: The umbrella driver processes the request:

```
// In AppiumDriver.createSession
const {driver: InnerDriver} = await this.driverConfig.findMatchingDriver
(desiredCaps);
// In this case, InnerDriver would be UiAutomator2Driver
const driverInstance = new InnerDriver(this.args, true);
const [innerSessionId, dCaps] = await driverInstance.createSession(...);
this.sessions[innerSessionId] = driverInstance;
```

Driver Hierarchy for Android Automation

When using the UiAutomator2 driver for Android automation in Appium, several key components work together behind the scenes to enable effective interaction with the device. At the center of this setup is the **UiAutomator2Driver**, a specialized Appium driver that implements UiAutomator2-specific commands and capabilities. This driver allows testers to perform advanced UI interactions on Android devices, such as scrolling through long lists, interacting with system-level UI components, and verifying complex UI states.

CHAPTER 11   CONTRIBUTE TO APPIUM

To support broader Android automation functionality, Appium also relies on the **AndroidDriver**, a general-purpose driver that offers a common interface for interacting with Android devices across multiple automation engines. This driver acts as a parent class for UiAutomator2Driver and provides shared logic and utility methods used in Android-based automation workflows.

Another essential component in the architecture is **ADB (Android Debug Bridge)**. ADB is a powerful command-line tool provided by the Android SDK that facilitates direct communication with Android devices or emulators. It handles tasks such as installing and uninstalling apps, retrieving system logs, executing shell commands, and port forwarding. Appium leverages ADB to prepare the device environment and manage lower-level operations during test execution.

Finally, the **UiAutomator2Server** plays a critical role as the execution engine on the device. This server is a lightweight Java application deployed to the device by Appium at runtime. Once deployed, it runs in the background and listens for automation commands sent from the Appium server. These commands are executed using Android's UiAutomator2 framework, which is part of the Android Testing Support Library and provides direct access to UI components at the OS level.

Together, these components UiAutomator2Driver, AndroidDriver, ADB, and UiAutomator2Server form the backbone of Appium's Android automation infrastructure. Understanding how they interact is essential for debugging issues, customizing driver behavior, and optimizing test reliability and performance.

Session Initialization Process

When `UiAutomator2Driver.createSession()` is called, the following steps occur:

1. Device Setup

    ```
    // The driver first sets up the Android device
    await this.startUiAutomator2Session(caps);
    ```

2. ADB Initialization

    ```
    // Initialize ADB and connect to the device
    this.adb = await ADB.createADB({
      javaVersion: this.opts.javaVersion,
      adbPort: this.opts.adbPort,
    ```

```
        remoteAdbHost: this.opts.remoteAdbHost,
        clearDeviceLogsOnStart: this.opts.clearDeviceLogsOnStart,
        adbExecTimeout: this.opts.adbExecTimeout,
});
```

3. Server Installation

   ```
   // Install the UiAutomator2 server app on the device if needed
   await this.installServerApk();
   ```

4. Server Startup

   ```
   // Start the UiAutomator2 server on the device
   await this.startUiAutomator2Server();
   // Establish a connection to the server
   await this.connectToUiAutomator2Server();
   ```

5. App Installation and Launch

   Install the app under test if provided; otherwise, the session begins with an application-less state in which it only works on the Android home screen.

   ```
   if (this.opts.app) {
      await this.installApp(this.opts.app);
   }
   // Launch the app
   await this.startApp();
   ```

Communication with the Device

When the client and the Appium server successfully establish a session from the createSession, the client(java) receives an identifier for this session request and then persists it in the driver instance to invoke any other session command. The server uses the session identifier as a mapping key to manage drivers. The test script follows a structured communication flow for each command. This flow begins with the client initiating an action—for example, a command like `driver.findElement(By.id("login_button")).click()` is sent to the Appium server. The server, acting as a central controller, receives this command and determines from the mappings is responsible for managing the active session. In the case of Android automation, this would typically be the `UiAutomator2Driver`. This driver plays a critical role in translating the incoming WebDriver command into a format that the `UiAutomator2` server on the device can understand. Once the command is translated, it is transmitted to the device where the `UiAutomator2` server is running. The server then uses Android's native `UiAutomator` framework to perform the requested action directly on the device's user interface. After the command is executed, a response—such as a success message or error—is generated and sent back along the same communication path: from the `UiAutomator2` server to the Appium server and finally back to the client. This seamless flow ensures that each command is accurately interpreted and executed in the context of the device's UI.

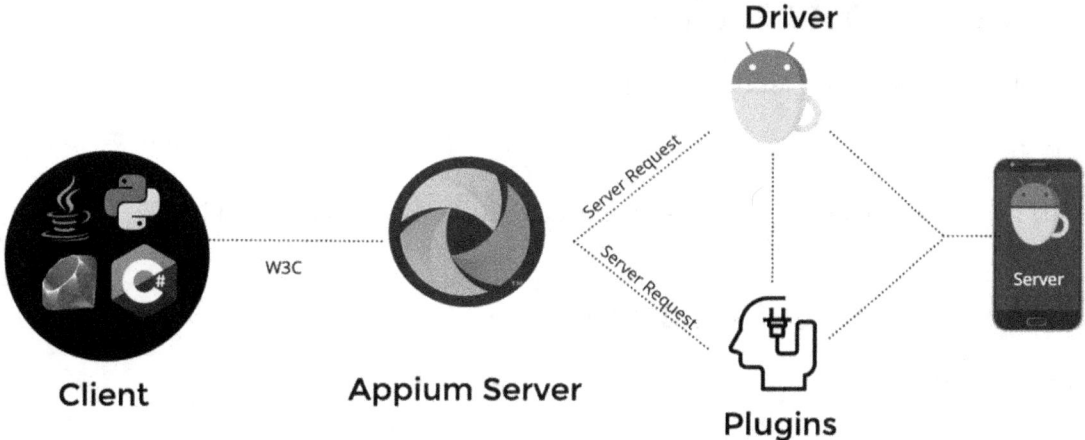

This multilayered architecture allows Appium to provide a consistent WebDriver interface while handling the complexities of different platforms behind the scenes.

Building Appium Locally

Now that we have gained a solid understanding of Appium's core internals and how the command flow operates—from the moment a command is issued by the client to the final response returned after device execution—we are well equipped to take the next step. In this section, we will explore how to work with the Appium codebase locally. This section includes setting up the Appium server environment on your machine, making custom modifications, and building the server from source. Additionally, we'll walk through the process of building an Appium driver locally. This approach is especially useful when you need to test changes, contribute to driver development, or debug specific issues. By compiling and running your version of the server and drivers, you gain full control over the behavior of Appium, enabling you to extend its capabilities or tailor it to specific testing needs. Let's dive into the steps involved in setting up and building Appium and its drivers locally.

1. Clone the Appium Repository

```
git clone https://github.com/appium/appium.git
cd appium
```

2. Install Dependencies

Install the necessary dependencies using npm:

```
npm install
```

This will install all the packages required to run and build Appium locally.

3. Build the Appium Server

```
npm run build
```

If everything goes well, then we have everything in place. You should see the logs as shown in Figure 11-1.

CHAPTER 11 CONTRIBUTE TO APPIUM

```
npm run build

> appium-monorepo@0.0.0 build
> run-s build:*


> appium-monorepo@0.0.0 build:compile
> tsc -b


> appium-monorepo@0.0.0 build:workspaces
> lerna run build

(node:94063) [DEP0040] DeprecationWarning: The `punycode` module is deprecated. Please use a userland alternative instead.
(Use `node --trace-deprecation ...` to show where the warning was created)
lerna notice cli v8.2.2
lerna info versioning independent
lerna info Executing command in 3 packages: "npm run build"
lerna info run Ran npm script 'build' in '@appium/schema' in 0.5s:

> @appium/schema@0.8.1 build
> node ./scripts/generate-schema-json.js

i Wrote JSON schema to /Users/saikrishna/Documents/git/appium/packages/schema/lib/appium-config.schema.json
✓ Done.
lerna info run Ran npm script 'build' in '@appium/fake-driver' in 0.5s:

> @appium/fake-driver@5.7.2 build
> cpy lib/screen.png build

lerna info run Ran npm script 'build' in '@appium/types' in 0.4s:

> @appium/types@0.25.3 build
> node ./scripts/generate-schema-types.js

i Wrote /Users/saikrishna/Documents/git/appium/packages/types/lib/appium-config.ts
✓ Done.
lerna success run Ran npm script 'build' in 3 packages in 0.9s:
lerna success - @appium/fake-driver
lerna success - @appium/schema
lerna success - @appium/types
```

Figure 11-1. Appium build logs

4. Clone and Build a Driver (e.g., UIAutomator2)

npm install will install all the dependencies, and npm run build will build the project. Refer to Figure 11-2.

CHAPTER 11   CONTRIBUTE TO APPIUM

```
git clone https://github.com/appium/appium-uiautomator2-driver.git
cd appium-uiautomator2-driver
npm install && npm run build
```

Figure 11-2. *Build project*

To verify that the Appium server is using your locally built version of a driver—such as the UiAutomator2Driver—you can insert a custom log message in the driver's source code. This simple but effective technique is particularly helpful when you're developing or debugging a driver and need to ensure your local changes are taking effect.

Let's walk through an example. Start by navigating to the source code of the driver you want to modify. In the case of the UiAutomator2 driver, the main driver logic typically resides in a file like lib/driver.js. Open this file and locate the createSession method or the class constructor—these are the places that get invoked when a new session starts.

```
console.log("💧 Using my locally modified UiAutomator2Driver!");
```

Every time you initiate a new session using this driver, the Appium server logs will print this message. It serves as a clear, visible indication that your custom-built driver is active.

Let's go ahead and build the appium-uiautomator2-driver. Run the below command from the appium-uiautomator2-driver path.

```
appium driver install --source=local --package=/path-to-your-driver
```

Once installed, the driver should appear in the list of drivers for dev mode.

CHAPTER 11 CONTRIBUTE TO APPIUM

```
appium driver list
✓ Listing available drivers
- uiautomator2@4.2.3 [installed (dev mode)]
- xcuitest [not installed]
- espresso [not installed]
- mac2 [not installed]
- windows [not installed]
- safari [not installed]
- gecko [not installed]
- chromium [not installed]
```

Let's start the Appium server and initiate an Android creation session from Appium Inspector to see our locally built driver. Refer to Figure 11-3.

```
[AppiumDriver@130a] Event 'newSessionRequested' logged at 1746790500758 (17:05:00 GMT+0530 (India Standard Time))
[BaseDriver] The capabilities ["platformName"] are standard capabilities and do not require "appium:" prefix
[Appium] Attempting to find matching driver for automationName 'UIAutomator2' and platformName 'android'
[Appium] The 'uiautomator2' driver was installed and matched caps.
[Appium] Will require it at /Users/saikrishna/Documents/git/appium-uiautomator2-driver
[Appium] Requiring driver at /Users/saikrishna/Documents/git/appium-uiautomator2-driver/build/index.js
[AppiumDriver@130a] Appium v2.18.0 creating new AndroidUiautomator2Driver (v4.2.3) session
[AppiumDriver@130a] Checking BaseDriver versions for Appium and AndroidUiautomator2Driver
[AppiumDriver@130a] Appium's BaseDriver version is 9.17.0
[AppiumDriver@130a] AndroidUiautomator2Driver's BaseDriver version is 9.17.0
[AndroidUiautomator2Driver@0485]
[AndroidUiautomator2Driver@0485] Creating session with W3C capabilities: {
  "alwaysMatch": {
    "appium:automationName": "UIAutomator2",
    "platformName": "android",
    "appium:newCommandTimeout": 3600,
    "appium:connectHardwareKeyboard": true
  },
  "firstMatch": [
    {}
  ]
}
[AndroidUiautomator2Driver@0485] The following provided capabilities were not recognized by this driver:
[AndroidUiautomator2Driver@0485]     connectHardwareKeyboard
[17ea4c79][AndroidUiautomator2Driver@0485] Session created with session id: 17ea4c79-9e37-4e89-b9c7-d18d8d3605df
[17ea4c79][ADB] Found 2 'build-tools' folders under '/Users/saikrishna/Library/Android/sdk' (newest first):
[17ea4c79][ADB]     /Users/saikrishna/Library/Android/sdk/build-tools/35.0.0
[17ea4c79][ADB]     /Users/saikrishna/Library/Android/sdk/build-tools/34.0.0
[17ea4c79][ADB] Using 'adb' from '/Users/saikrishna/Library/Android/sdk/platform-tools/adb'
[17ea4c79][ADB] Running '/Users/saikrishna/Library/Android/sdk/platform-tools/adb -P 5037 start-server'
[17ea4c79][AndroidUiautomator2Driver@0485] Retrieving device list
[17ea4c79][ADB] Trying to find connected Android devices
[17ea4c79][ADB] Getting connected devices
[17ea4c79][ADB] Connected devices: [{"udid":"emulator-5554","state":"device"}]
[17ea4c79][AndroidUiautomator2Driver@0485] Using device: emulator-5554
[17ea4c79][ADB] Using 'adb' from '/Users/saikrishna/Library/Android/sdk/platform-tools/adb'
[17ea4c79][ADB] Running '/Users/saikrishna/Library/Android/sdk/platform-tools/adb -P 5037 start-server'
[17ea4c79][ADB] Setting device id to emulator-5554
[17ea4c79][AndroidUiautomator2Driver@0485] 🔥 Using my locally modified UiAutomator2Driver!
[17ea4c79][AndroidUiautomator2Driver@0485] Neither 'app' nor 'appPackage' was set. Starting UiAutomator2 without the target application
```

Figure 11-3. *Logs with custom log*

CHAPTER 11   CONTRIBUTE TO APPIUM

Summary

In this chapter, we explored the practical aspects of working with Appium's source code and drivers in a local development environment. We began by understanding the internal command flow of an Appium session, starting from the client sending a command to the Appium server routing it through the appropriate driver, down to the device for execution, and finally back to the client with a response.

Building on this foundational understanding, we moved into hands-on development by setting up Appium locally. We walked through the steps to clone the Appium server and a specific driver (like UiAutomator2), install dependencies, build the code, and link the components together. We then demonstrated how to make a simple but effective change to the driver, adding a custom log message to confirm it is being used during test sessions.

Finally, we used Appium Inspector to initiate a real Android session using the modified driver. This procedure not only provided a graphical interface to interact with the app but also offered visual and log-based confirmation that the locally built driver was active. The appearance of our custom log messages in the Appium server logs validated the success of our development and integration efforts.

By the end of this chapter, you should feel confident in setting up, modifying, and testing both the Appium server and its drivers locally. This capability is especially valuable for contributing to the Appium open source ecosystem, debugging issues, or tailoring drivers to meet specific testing needs.

CHAPTER 12

Integrating Appium Tests in Continuous Integration (CI) Pipelines

What Will You Learn

In this chapter, we will explore how to integrate your Appium tests into continuous integration (CI) pipelines using popular CI tools like GitHub Actions. CI is a crucial part of modern software development and test automation workflows, especially for mobile applications where builds and tests need to be run frequently and reliably across multiple devices and platforms.

The Importance of CI in Mobile Test Automation

Running Appium tests manually or on an ad hoc basis is inefficient and error-prone and does not scale. Integrating your tests with CI pipelines ensures that

- **Bugs Are Caught Early**: Automated Appium tests can be triggered with every code commit, build, or pull request.
- **Developers Get Instant Feedback**: If something breaks, CI notifies the team, helping maintain high product quality.
- **Automation Becomes Reliable**: You build a consistent and repeatable way to validate Android and iOS app behavior.
- **Your QA Cycles Accelerate**: CI reduces the time between development and testing, helping teams move faster.

CHAPTER 12   INTEGRATING APPIUM TESTS IN CONTINUOUS INTEGRATION (CI) PIPELINES

This chapter helps you move from manual or local test execution to **automated and continuous test feedback**.

How to Run Appium Tests in GitHub Actions

CI platforms like GitHub Actions require a carefully defined configuration to run Appium tests reliably in a headless and automated environment. One of the first steps is learning how to define workflows using .yml files, which instruct GitHub Actions on when and how to execute your test jobs, such as triggering the test suite on every push or pull request. Within these workflows, you'll configure steps to install all the necessary dependencies including Node.js, Appium, Java (for Java-based test clients), and any additional tools or libraries your test framework requires. A critical part of mobile automation is simulating real device conditions, so you'll also learn how to set up and launch Android emulators and iOS simulators in the CI environment, ensuring they are booted, unlocked, and ready before tests begin. Finally, once the tests are complete, it's important to preserve visibility in the results.

Android GitHub Actions YAML

Let's consider the GitHub Actions .yml file below for Android test run.

```
name: Android Tests
on:
  pull_request:
    branches: [main]

jobs:
  test:
    runs-on: ubuntu-24.04
    strategy:
      matrix:
        api-level: [30]
        target: [default]

    steps:
      - name: checkout
        uses: actions/checkout@v4
```

```yaml
- name: Install Appium and UIAutomator2 Driver
  run: |
    npm install -g appium
    appium driver install uiautomator2

- name: Enable KVM
  run: |
    echo 'KERNEL=="kvm", GROUP="kvm", MODE="0666", OPTIONS+="static_node=kvm"' | sudo tee /etc/udev/rules.d/99-kvm4all.rules
    sudo udevadm control --reload-rules
    sudo udevadm trigger --name-match=kvm

- name: Start Appium Server in Background
  run: |
    nohup appium --base-path /wd/hub > appium.log 2>&1 &
    echo "Waiting for Appium server to start..."
    for i in {1..30}; do
      if curl -s http://localhost:4723/wd/hub/status | grep -q '"ready":true'; then
        echo "Appium server is ready."
        break
      fi
      echo "Waiting..."
      sleep 2
    done

- name: run health check
  id: health_check
  run: |
    npm run test-e2e-health

- name: run tests
  uses: reactivecircus/android-emulator-runner@v2
  with:
    api-level: ${{ matrix.api-level }}
    target: ${{ matrix.target }}
    arch: x86_64
```

CHAPTER 12   INTEGRATING APPIUM TESTS IN CONTINUOUS INTEGRATION (CI) PIPELINES

```
        profile: Nexus 6
        script: npm run test-e2e-android
```

Trigger Section

```
on:
  pull_request:
    branches: [main]
```

Explanation

- This section defines when the workflow should run.

- It is triggered **automatically when a pull request targets the main branch**.

- This ensures tests are executed for every PR before it gets merged, maintaining quality.

Jobs Section

```
jobs:
  test:
    runs-on: ubuntu-24.04
```

Explanation

- It defines a single job called a "test."

- It runs on a GitHub-hosted Ubuntu 24.04 virtual machine.

- This VM is isolated per workflow run and comes with essential development tools preinstalled.

Test Matrix Strategy

```
    strategy:
      matrix:
        api-level: [30]
        target: [default]
```

CHAPTER 12   INTEGRATING APPIUM TESTS IN CONTINUOUS INTEGRATION (CI) PIPELINES

Explanation

- A matrix allows running tests against different configurations.
- Currently, it tests only Android API level 30 with the default system image.
- You can scale this to include multiple API levels or targets.

Steps Section

Checkout Source Code

```
- name: checkout
  uses: actions/checkout@v4
```

Install Appium and UIAutomator2 Driver

```
- name: Install Appium and UIAutomator2 Driver
  run: |
    npm install -g appium
    appium driver install uiautomator2
```

- Installs Appium globally using npm.
- Then installs the uiautomator2 driver, which is used for automating Android devices.

Enable KVM (Virtualization)

```
- name: Enable KVM
  run: |
    echo 'KERNEL=="kvm", GROUP="kvm", MODE="0666", OPTIONS+="static_node=kvm"' | sudo tee /etc/udev/rules.d/99-kvm4all.rules
    sudo udevadm control --reload-rules
    sudo udevadm trigger --name-match=kvm
```

- **KVM (kernel-based virtual machine)** enhances emulator performance.
- This step ensures the Ubuntu runner has permission to use KVM.
- Without this, the Android emulator would be extremely slow or fail to launch.

CHAPTER 12 INTEGRATING APPIUM TESTS IN CONTINUOUS INTEGRATION (CI) PIPELINES

Start Appium Server and Wait Until Ready

```
- name: Start Appium Server in Background
  run: |
    nohup appium --base-path /wd/hub > appium.log 2>&1 &
    echo "Waiting for Appium server to start..."
    for i in {1..30}; do
      if curl -s http://localhost:4723/wd/hub/status | grep -q
      '"ready":true'; then
        echo "Appium server is ready."
        break
      fi
      echo "Waiting..."
      sleep 2
    done
```

- Starts the Appium server **in the background.**

- Logs output to `appium.log`.

- A loop checks Appium's `/status` endpoint every two seconds (up to 30 tries).

- The test job continues only once Appium reports `"ready": true`.

Launch Emulator and Run Android Tests

```
- name: run tests
  uses: reactivecircus/android-emulator-runner@v2
  with:
    api-level: ${{ matrix.api-level }}
    target: ${{ matrix.target }}
    arch: x86_64
    profile: Nexus 6
    script: npm run test-e2e-android
```

CHAPTER 12   INTEGRATING APPIUM TESTS IN CONTINUOUS INTEGRATION (CI) PIPELINES

- Uses the community-supported `android-emulator-runner` GitHub Action.

- Boots an Android emulator with

  - API level 30.

  - x86_64 architecture.

  - Device profile: `Nexus 6`.

- Once booted, runs your test suite using the npm command `test-e2e-android`.

- The emulator is shut down automatically after the tests are complete.

So far, we have explored how to configure Android emulators within a GitHub Actions workflow. This included installing Appium and ensuring that the Appium server is fully operational before triggering any test executions. Setting up the Android environment in CI is an essential step for automating test cases and maintaining a consistent test pipeline.

Now, let's shift our focus to iOS. In the upcoming section, we'll walk through the process of configuring iOS simulators in GitHub Actions. This will include setting up the required macOS runner, installing the necessary dependencies such as Xcode command-line tools, and launching an iOS simulator. We'll also ensure that the Appium server is correctly started and ready to handle test sessions before any tests are executed. By the end of this section, you'll have a fully functional CI setup that supports both Android and iOS automated testing.

iOS GitHub YAML File

```
name: iOS Tests

on:
  pull_request:
    branches: [main]

jobs:
  test:
    runs-on: macos-latest
```

```yaml
    strategy:
      matrix:
        ios-version: ["18.1"]
        device: ["iPhone 16"]

    steps:
      - name: Checkout source code
        uses: actions/checkout@v4

      - name: Setup Node.js
        uses: actions/setup-node@v3
        with:
          node-version: "18"
          cache: "npm"

      - name: Install dependencies
        run: npm install

      - name: Build project
        run: npm run build-webpack

      - name: List available simulators
        run: xcrun simctl list devices available

      - name: List iOS runtimes
        run: |
          brew install xq
          xcrun simctl list runtimes
          xcrun --sdk iphonesimulator --show-sdk-version

      - name: Prepare iOS simulator
        id: prepareSimulator
        uses: futureware-tech/simulator-action@v4
        with:
          model: "iPhone 16"
          os_version: "18.1"
          shutdown_after_job: false
          wait_for_boot: true
```

```
      - name: Run iOS tests
        run: |
          ./node_modules/.bin/appium driver run xcuitest build-wda --sdk=
          "18.1" --name="iPhone 16"
          npm run test-e2e-ios
```

Workflow Trigger

```
name: iOS Testt
on:
  pull_request:
    branches: [main]
```

Explanation:

- name: Sets a friendly name for this workflow.
- on: Defines when the workflow is triggered.
- pull_request: ensures this workflow runs every time a pull request targets the main branch.This is useful for catching bugs in iOS-specific code before merging to the main codebase.

Jobs and Strategy

```
jobs:
  test:
    runs-on: macos-latest
    strategy:
      matrix:
        ios-version: ["18.1"]
        device: ["iPhone 16"]
```

Explanation

- **jobs:** defines a single job named test.
- **runs-on: macos-latest** tells GitHub to provision a **macOS** runner– required for iOS testing.

- **matrix:** allows testing against multiple configurations (e.g., multiple iOS versions or devices).
  - In this case, it uses **iOS 18.1** and **iPhone 16**.
  - This setup is scalable–you can add more device types or iOS versions later.

List Available Simulators

```
- run: xcrun simctl list devices available
  name: List Installed Simulators
```

- Lists all available simulators on the macOS runner
- Helpful for debugging if the desired simulator isn't found

List iOS Runtimes and SDK Version

```
- run: |
    brew install xq
    xcrun simctl list runtimes
    xcrun --sdk iphonesimulator --show-sdk-version
  name: List Runtimes
```

- Installs xq (a jq-like XML processor) that may be useful for parsing output
- Lists all iOS runtimes installed
- Shows the simulator SDK version (e.g., 18.1)
- Helps confirm if your target simulator and SDK are available on the runner

Prepare iOS Simulator

```
- name: Prepare iOS simulator
  id: prepareSimulator
  uses: futureware-tech/simulator-action@v4
  with:
    model: "iPhone 16"
    os_version: "18.1"
    shutdown_after_job: false
    wait_for_boot: true
```

CHAPTER 12   INTEGRATING APPIUM TESTS IN CONTINUOUS INTEGRATION (CI) PIPELINES

- Uses a prebuilt GitHub Action to
  - Boot the **iPhone 16 simulator** with **iOS 18.1**.
  - You can optionally shut it down after the job ends; selecting false allows you to continue using it.
  - Waits until the simulator is fully booted.
- This avoids flaky test failures due to simulators not being ready.

Run Appium and Execute iOS Tests

```
name: Run iOS tests
  run: |
    ./node_modules/.bin/appium driver run xcuitest build-wda --sdk="18.1" --name="iPhone 16"
    npm run test-e2e-ios
```

a. `build-wda` Step

- The XCUITest driver is used to **build WebDriverAgent (WDA)** for the selected simulator.
- This is essential–WDA is the bridge between Appium and the iOS device/simulator.

b. `npm run test-e2e-ios`

- Runs your actual end-to-end (E2E) test suite for iOS.
- This command should
  - Connect to the running simulator.
  - Use the running Appium server.
  - Execute all tests defined in your test framework (e.g., WDIO, Mocha, Jest).

CHAPTER 12   INTEGRATING APPIUM TESTS IN CONTINUOUS INTEGRATION (CI) PIPELINES

Summary

In this chapter, we learned how to set up the Appium server within a GitHub Actions workflow. We walked through the process of configuring Android and iOS devices, including starting emulators and simulators in a macOS environment. We also ensured that the Appium server is properly started and ready before any tests are executed. Finally, we integrated a test automation framework and enabled it to run as part of the GitHub Actions pipeline. With this setup, your mobile tests can now run automatically on every code change, helping to maintain quality and catch issues early.

Index

A

ADB, *see* Android Debug Bridge (ADB)
Android application, 183
    client-side initialization, 183, 184
    driver hierarchy, 184, 185
    emulators/real devices, 18
    events, 184
    GitHub actions, 194–199
    Mac
        configuration, 23
        device hardware, 21
        download, 20
        empty project, 19
        installation, 19
        navigation, 23
        system image, 22
        test automation, 23, 24
        virtual device, 20, 21
    modules, 18
    wdio.android.conf.ts, 101
    wdio.conf.ts file, 100–105
    Windows
        ANDROID_HOME, 26
        emulators, 26, 27
        environment variables, 24, 25
        setup, 25
        system properties, 24
Android, architecture, 5
Android automation
    prerequisites, 15
Android Debug Bridge (ADB), 108, 185
    android devices, 45
    communication, 44
    connection, 45
    developer options, 44
    device, 45
    USB debugging, 44
Android Virtual Device (AVD), 75
API, *see* Application programming interface (API)
Appium 3.0
    Android (*see* Android application)
    Android-specific prerequisites, 15
    automation tools, 1
    client-server architecture, 4
        architecture, 5
        client-to-device process flow, 6
        workflow, 5
    definition, 3
    driver installation, 8
    drivers, 8, 30–36
    extensibility/platforms, 4
    general prerequisites, 14
    growth/community, 2
    independent modules, 9
    installation process, 9
    iOS Auto, 1
    iOS-Specific Prerequisites, 15
    logs, 107–125
    mobile application, 3
    modular driver architecture, 11
    open source release/evolution, 2
    pligin (*see* Plugins)
    pluggable drivers, 8

INDEX

Appium 3.0 (*cont.*)
   plugin
      architecture, 6
      intercepts, 7
      key benefits, 10, 11
      team/community, 9, 10
      workflow, 7
   prerequisites/setup steps, 13
   project naming, 2
   responsibilities, 8
   Selenium conference, 2
   server (*see* Server installation)
   setup process, 13
   standardization, 3
   streamlined configuration, 11
   testing process, 1
   UIAutomation framework, 1
   WebDriver protocol, 3
AppiumDriver, 170–172
Application programming interface (API)
   gestures, 128, 129
AVD, *see* Android Virtual Device (AVD)

B

BaseDriver, 172–174
BiDi (bidirectional) command, 175
Bidirectional (BiDi) communication, 182

C

CLI, *see* Command Line Interfaces (CLI)
Cloud devices (LambdaTest)
   account, 79
   advantages, 78
   capabilities, 82
   capability generator tool, 80
   credentials, 79, 80

   desired capabilities, 80
   retrieve steps, 79
   uploading app, 81, 82
Command execution flow, 177, 178
Command Line Interfaces (CLI), 145
Communication, 186, 187
Context management
   debugging, 164
   key consideration, 164
   native context, 162
   native/web-based components, 161
   switching elements, 164
   test execution, 162
   W3C WebDriver specification, 162
   web automation techniques, 163
   web-based content, 162
   WebView, 162
   XCUITest driver, 163
Continuous integration (CI)
   GitHub actions (*see* GitHub actions)
   mobile test automation, 193, 194
   pipelines, 193
Core architecture
   AppiumDriver, 170–172
   BaseDriver, 172–174
   DriverCore, 174, 175
   ExtensionCore, 175, 176
   inheritance pattern, 170

D

Desired capabilities
   appium-specific capabilities, 64
   cloud platforms, 65
   cloud providers, 65
   definition, 63
   fundamentals, 63
   mandatory capabilities, 65

INDEX

parallel test execution
    approaches, 66, 68
    parallel execution, 67
    per-request approach, 67
    pre-processes, 66
    scenarios, 68
    session/device, 67
standard protocol, 64
DriverCore, 174, 175
Drivers
    appium driver list, 31
    community, 33–35
    dev mode, 35
    dev team, 31, 32
    extension system, 179, 180
    flutter integration, 32
    installation, 30, 31
    server execution
        clone repository, 188
        dependencies, 188
        dev mode, 190
        logs, 189, 191
        project, 189, 190
    testing process, 34–36
    XCUITest driver, 31

E, F

ExtensionCore, 175, 176
Extension system, 179

G

Gestures, 127
    abstractions, 131
    client libraries, 128
    debugging methods, 133
    horizontal swipe gesture, 129

    key elements, 129, 130
    mobile app, 132
    multitouch interactions, 128
    perform() method, 128
    plugin ecosystem, 132
    step-by-step process, 130, 131
    WebDriver, 127
GitHub actions
    android YAML code, 194–199
    configuration, 194
    emulator/tests, 198
    iOS YAML file, 199–203
    jobs/strategy, 201
    KVM (Virtualization), 197
    mobile automation, 194
    server, 198
    simulators, 202
    steps section, 197
    test matrix strategy, 196

H

HTTP, *see* Hypertext transfer protocol (HTTP)
Hypertext transfer protocol (HTTP), 181

I

Inspect elements, 71
    attributes panel, 84
    element interaction, 89–92
    element selection, 83, 84
    exploring option, 82
    installation, 71–73
    iOS applications/android, 73–82
    locator strategies, 84
    mobile app hierarchy, 83
    search icon, 89

Inspect elements (*cont.*)
  session builder screen, 72
  unreliable strategies, 84
iOS application
  command-line tool path, 30–32
  creation, 1
  gestures, 132
  GitHub YAML file, 199–203
  inspect elements, 73
    android capabilities, 74
    attributes panel, 85, 86
    basic syntax, 86
    capabilities, 73, 76
    cloud devices, 78–82
    deviceName/platformVersion, 76
    finding multiple elements, 87
    logical operators, 87
    predicates, 88
    predicate string, 86
    preferred strategies, 88
    server logs, 77
    session builder, 73
    session creation, 75, 77
    string matching, 86
    terminal and run command, 73
    unreliable strategies, 88
    WebDriverAgent, 87
  performance optimization, 153–157
  platform dependency, 27
  real device, 45
    components, 49
    developer section, 47
    settings app, 46
    trust device, 46
    WebView automation, 48
  server logs, 116–125
  simulator, 27
  specific Prerequisites, 15

wdio.conf.ts file, 100–105
wdio.ios.conf.ts, 101
workflow, 5
Xcode installation, 28, 29

J

Java Development Kit (JDK)
  download/installation, 16
  installation, 17
  JAVA_HOME setup, 17
  Mac/Linux, 16
  Windows, 16
JDK, *see* Java Development Kit (JDK)

K

Kernel-based virtual machine (KVM), 197
KVM, *see* Kernel-based virtual machine (KVM)

L

Logs
  essential tool, 107
  modules, 108
  structured format, 107

M

Monorepo structure, 169
Multilayered architecture, 187

N

Node.js, 15
Node Package Manager (NPM), 13
NPM, *see* Node Package Manager (NPM)

O

Optimization
    contexts (*see* Context management)
    desired location, 159
    element, 159, 160
    handling OTP, 158
    MJPEG server, 161
    multiple screenshots, 160
    tapElement, 160
    tapElementPosition, 160
    WebDriverAgent (WDA), 153–157
One-time password (OTP)
    implementation, 158
    W3C actions, 158

P, Q

Plugins
    architecture, 6, 7
    benefits, 11
    CLI arguments, 145
    dev team, 9, 10
    Doctor
        command-line utility, 40
        terminal code, 41, 42
        troubleshooting process, 41
        working process, 41
    extension system, 180
    installation, 36, 37
        community, 38, 39
        dev team, 37
        GitHub repository, 39
        testing process, 39, 40
    intercept commands
        array, 139
        command names, 138
        driver instance, 139
        handling command, 138
        method parameters, 138–140
    interception/handle method, 140
        error methods, 142
        execution time, 141–145
        findElement command, 142
        overrides, 140
    key benefits, 10, 11
    overloading execution
        execute method, 148–151
        executeMethodMap, 148
        executeScript, 150
        scripts, 147
        test script, 150
        WebDriver, 147
    project creation
        index.js file, 137
        installation, 137
        Node.js project, 136
        package.json, 136
    scripts, 150
    sever process, 135
    terminal/run command, 36
    traditional HTTP interface, 135

R

React native app, 165
    conflicts, 166
    platform-specific mapping, 165
    platform strategies, 167
    separation of concerns, 166
    testID/accessibilityLabel map, 165
    test suite dependability, 165
    validation workflow, 167
Real device configuration
    ADB real devices, 44, 45
    emulators, 43

Real device configuration (*cont.*)
    iOS automation, 45–49
    learning process, 43, 44
    WebDriverAgent, 50–61
Routing, 181

S

Server installation
    terminal/command prompt, 17, 18
    verify installation, 18
Server logs, 107
    ADB initialization/device detection, 111, 112
    appium-uiautomator2-server, 113, 114
    arguments/configuration, 108
    client commands, 114–116
    connection URLs, 110
    driver loading, 109
    drivers and plugins, 110
    home path detection, 109
    HTTP interface initialization, 109
    initialization, 108
    iOS application
        BaseDriver, 119
        client commands, 123–125
        drivers, 117
        home path, 117
        initialization, 116
        platformVersion, 120
        session creation process, 118
        WebDriverAgent (WDA), 120–123
        XCUITestDriver, 119
    locator strategies, 115
    session creation, 110, 111
    See also Logs
Session initialization process, 185, 186
Session management, 182

T, U, V

Troubleshooting, *see* Optimization

W, X, Y, Z

WDA, *see* WebDriverAgent (WDA)
WDIO, *see* WebdriverIO (WDIO)
WebDriver, 147
    gestures, 127
WebDriverAgent (WDA), 116
    appium-xcuitest-driver, 50
    automation commands, 50
    client commands, 123–125
    developer certificate, 52
    development team, 51
    device management, 52, 53
    generic devices, 54–61
    iOS application, 87
    navigation, 54–61
    optimization
        code signing setup, 154, 155
        configuration, 154
        go-ios installation, 156
        initialization and connectivity, 155
        installation, 156
        Node.js, 155
        port forward, 156
        pre-build session, 154
        XCUITest driver package, 154
    server logs, 120–123
    testing framework, 53
    working process, 50
    Xcode application, 51
WebdriverIO (WDIO)
    configuration file
        dependencies folder, 98
        key files and folders, 98

package.json file, 99
package-lpck.json, 100
test scripts, 98
tsconfig.json, 100
wdio.conf.js file, 99
wizard setup, 97
dependencies/configurations, 95
dependency installation, 96
environment variables, 95
Node.js project, 96
package.json, 96
project setup, 95
selectors, 104
service dependencies, 96
wdio.conf.ts file, 100–105
WebDriver protocol, 3

GPSR Compliance

The European Union's (EU) General Product Safety Regulation (GPSR) is a set of rules that requires consumer products to be safe and our obligations to ensure this.

If you have any concerns about our products, you can contact us on

ProductSafety@springernature.com

In case Publisher is established outside the EU, the EU authorized representative is:

Springer Nature Customer Service Center GmbH
Europaplatz 3
69115 Heidelberg, Germany